Wisdom at Work

Let Davidson, Ph.D., is a global corporate consultant, leadership coach, and retreat leader. A student of the Perennial Philosophy for thirty years, Let specializes in translating core teachings and practices of the world's spiritual, philosophic, and psychological traditions into daily life, work, and organizations.

Since 1980 he has given hundreds of seminars on empowerment, stress and change management, and personal and spiritual development throughout the U.S. His regular clients have included Corning Incorporated, Cornell University, and Carondolet Management Institute, in addition to a wide range of small businesses, hospitals, and school districts.

Let currently coaches leaders and presents Wisdom at Work retreats on the awakening of leadership in the workplace. For more information on Let's work and retreats, contact him by e-mail at dasarath@baka.com or through the Larson Publications web site http://www.lightlink.com/larson/

WISDOM
at Work

The
Awakening
of
Consciousness
in the
Workplace

Let Davidson, Ph.D.

Published for the Paul Brunton Philosophic Foundation by
LARSON PUBLICATIONS

International Standard Book Number: 0-943914-86-8
Library of Congress Catalog Card Number: 98-65813

Published for the Paul Brunton Philosophic Foundation by
Larson Publications
4936 NYS Route 414
Burdett, New York 14818 USA

Publisher and author gratefully acknowledge the following permissions to reprint material under copyright:

Page 51 from: THE POETRY OF ROBERT FROST, edited by Edward Connery Lathem, Copyright 1936, © 1964 by Lesly Frost Ballantine, © 1969 by Henry Holt and Company, Inc., © 1997 by Edward Connery Lathem. Reprinted by permission of Henry Holt and Company, Inc.

Page 87 from *God as Nature Sees God*, A Christian Reading of the Tao Te Ching (Element, 1994). Copyright © John R. Mabry 1994. Used by permission.

Page 89 from *The Ring of the Way*, by Taisen Deshimaru, translated by Nancy Amphoux, Translation copyright © 1983 by Editions Cesare Rancilio. Translation copyright © 1987 by E.P. Dutton. Used by permission of Dutton, a division of Penguin Putnam Inc.

Designed by Milenda Nan Ok Lee
Set in Adobe Caslon

05 04 03 02 01 00 99 98

10 9 8 7 6 5 4 3 2 1

To Papaji,

Beloved Master,

H.W.L. Poonja, 1910–1997

with immeasurable gratitude for the impossible gift

CONTENTS

ACKNOWLEDGMENTS

I want to thank my editor Paul Cash for graciously bringing order, clarity, and flow to a huge amount of material, and for his patience and unfailing good will toward a finicky writer.

I also wish to express my gratitude to Timothy Smith, who first suggested I had a book in me and for his wise counsel to resume it every time I wanted to let it go; to all the members of the Wisdom_at_Work Internet discussion group which I moderated 1995–1997, whose lively and profound e-mail conversation triggered the first drafts of much of this writing and the idea of the book; and to Karen Speerstra for her encouragement to write a book and her editorial advice on earlier attempts at organization.

To my colleagues: Judi Neal of the Center for the Spirit at Work for her love and encouragement; Jeffrey Mishlove for his generous support of my writing on the Intuition Network online groups; Alex Pattakos, formerly president of Renaissance Business Associates for giving me the opportunity to write for the RBA newsletter and sponsoring Wisdom_at_Work online; Marcus Robinson for his friendship and allowing me to publish some of this material on his web site; Copthorne MacDonald for posting my first article on his web site; Martin Rutte, James Berry, and Marty Raphael for giving me the opportunity to discuss these ideas at the Second Annual International Conference on

Spirituality in Business; Joel Metzger for encouraging me to publish electronically on his Online Noetic Network; and Gigi Van Deckter for her heartfelt intuitive counsel and urging to be myself.

To my dear *dharma* friends: David Mulveny, for our ongoing dialogue on freedom; Hanuman, for his impassioned urging to publish and all our conversations on the reality underlying this work; Mitch Bobrow for his enthusiastic support; Gangaji, true heart sister, for her playful, unconditional encouragement and sharing of truth; and to Richard Lal Gordon, for three decades of sharing the mystery together and always validating my attempts at integration in the world.

To my friend and colleague Bonnie Harrison for opening many doors for my work at Cornell University and Corning Incorporated; Charles Craig, Lina Echeverría, Jacques LeMoine, Dr. Joseph Mathey, Eve Menger, Jeff Monroy, Randy Schiavone, Jim Scott, and Keith Vaughan for encouraging the work at Corning, and Garry and Sherry de Rose and the staff of the College Center of the Finger Lakes; Judy Acheson, Mick Ellis, Ellen Ely, Jared Harrison, Ron Loomis, Louise Maynard, Mike Nunno, Rob Osborn, Dennis Osika, John Rudan, and Jean Samuelson for supporting my work so graciously at Cornell University; Marilyn Draxl, Linda Vincent, and the staff at Conceptual Systems Inc. for the opportunity to coach leaders; Joseph McCollough, Susan Villaescusa, Ann Fortune, and the staff at Carondelet Management Institute for sending me to five hundred cities nationally to try out many of these ideas in their seminars; Paul Deslauriers and Christine Warner of New Resources for Growth for long discussions on consciousness and our good work together; and Gloria Cox, Treasure Miller, and the managers of Harbin Hot Springs for allowing me to work so closely with them on their noble experiment to create a truly conscious organization.

I would also like to acknowledge my teachers whose influence shows up in this book: to Richard Morse, for revealing to me the secret spirit and meaning of history, and to Philip Curtin for teaching me the craft of history; to Robert Youngblood, David Allen, and the Insight Consulting Group for their lucid teachings on the inner technology of change; and to Peter Block for demonstrating mastery as a consultant who lives spirit in his work.

To my spiritual teachers: Swami Satchidananda who started me on a lifetime of yoga study; to Werner Erhard and the *est* trainers, who showed me a glimpse of the ancient wisdom integrated in a modern life; to my Vipassana teachers N.S. Goenka, Joseph Goldstein, and Alan Clements who taught mindfulness; to Joshu Sasaki Roshi who so boldly manifested the reality of Zen; and, most of all, to my beloved master H.W.L. Poonja—Papaji—whose presence lives in every word of this book.

Finally, I am deeply grateful to Barbara, my wife, spiritual companion, and teacher for almost twenty-five years, for her patient support and counsel, and for allowing me the space to do my work within our loving family life.

Wisdom is the principal thing; therefore, get wisdom,

and with all thy getting, get understanding.

Exalt her, and she shall promote thee:

she shall bring thee to honor, when thou dost embrace her.

She shall give to thine head an ornament of grace:

A crown of glory shall she deliver to thee.

—Proverbs 4:7–9

Here is the test of wisdom,

Wisdom is not tested in schools,

Wisdom cannot be pass'd from one having it to another not having it,

Wisdom is of the soul, is not susceptible of proof, has its own proof,

Applies to all stages and objects and qualities and its content,

Is the certainty of the reality and immortality of things,

 and the excellence of things;

Something there is in the float of the sight of things

 That provokes it out of the soul.

—Walt Whitman, *Leaves of Grass*

What we learn after we know it all is what counts.

—Seneca

I

INTRODUCTION

Awakening

This book is about awakening: an awakening to the fullness of who we are and how our whole self can be integrated in our daily work.

For the past thirty years, as an historian, organizational trainer, consultant, and leadership coach, I sought to bridge what seemed like two irreconcilably separate worlds. In this attempt I took heart in knowing that even the great American Transcendentalist, Ralph Waldo Emerson, grappled with integrating the timeless domain of spirit with the busy life of work:

> The worst feature of this double consciousness is, that the two lives, of the [activity] and of the soul, which we lead, really show very little relation to each other; one prevails now, all buzz and din; and the other prevails then, all infinitude and paradise; and with the progress of life, the two discover no greater disposition to reconcile themselves.

In pursuing this integration I have lived with these central questions:

Can our work be a place of transformation, spiritual growth, and, ultimately, self-realization?

How can we experience and express fulfillment through our work of earning a living?

What do self-awareness and love look like in the work setting?

Can we revitalize our organizations and shape them in harmony with our values and deepest truth?

How can we create meaningful, satisfying work and conscious, healthy organizations?

What will motivate people to take charge of their happiness, satisfaction, and high performance at work?

What challenges and controversies surround the discussion of spirituality in the work setting?

And, most recently: What is the role of cyberspace in this whole process?

I describe here the different approaches I have taken to answering these questions and discovering this union. They all touch on how I have been applying principles and techniques of the Perennial Philosophy—the core wisdom of the world's psychological, spiritual, and philosophical traditions—to the workplace and corporate life. They draw upon three decades of personal study and practice in the wisdom traditions of east and west, in which I have been fortunate to work with masters in Zen, Yoga, Vipassana, Advaita Vedanta, and contemporary American traditions of enlightenment and practice, as well as investigating my native Judæo-Christian heritage.

During these years I have come to see the workplace as a legitimate domain for the awakening of consciousness and the activity of spirit. I learned that there is a peace, self-knowledge, and happiness that can be known and lived in everyday life and work, that it is possible to realize our deepest self in the context of our organizations and businesses.

Inquiry & Dialogue

I have recently realized how much I love to share this process with people. I most enjoy creating intimate relationship and engaging people in a sincere, heartfelt inquiry into how this realization can be experienced at work. We establish honest dialogue, talk about how important it is to be open, and become aware of the challenges involved with translating our views. I have been especially attentive to developing a language that includes as many people as possible and provides a common ground for sharing our most intimate experience. This often leads to true dialogue where the medium really is the message—that is, the communication process itself becomes the communion, not necessarily the acceptance of a certain point of view or attainment of a specific outcome.

The real task I see facing us, as individuals aspiring to live our deepest truth as well as professionals committed to supporting change in the workplace, is to integrate wisdom and work, the spiritual and the practical, to bring the sky to the road and the heart to the marketplace. Can we find the common ground of the bean counter and the dreamer, of those who require measurement, logic, and proof, and those who know by intuiting and feeling? Can we merge the drive for productive work and the inner necessity to love and commune with one another?

Given the volatile mix of possibilities now interacting unpredictably in our world, it seems essential that we do so. Consciousness does seem to be revealing itself progressively—at least for certain segments of the population—in an emergent holistic and unitive vision of life and work. But are we willing to heal the dualistic split that fragments the person into an object of production, and to allow the whole being into our work? Are we willing to integrate our inner and outer lives and see our work as a place of making a meaningful living and encouraging individual fulfillment and freedom? Is leadership enlightened enough to rise to the occasion and recognize the opportunity?

And, if we are to pursue this authentically, are we willing to deal with the Pandora's box of conflicting views and resistance that will most likely accompany attempts to address these issues at work? How can we preserve the essential pluralism, diversity, and tolerance of our society and at the same time discuss the deepest beliefs and values in people's lives?

Are we ready to participate in a dialogue—already beginning to arise in American society—as the necessary context for expanded consciousness? Will we face one another and honestly discuss the differences and common ground between secular humanist and religious views, between liberal and fundamentalist approaches, between universalist and dogmatic only-way beliefs, between dualistic and unitive modes of consciousness? How will we deal with those who consider it inappropriate to engage any of these concerns at work? Or with those who seek to impose only their way?

It seems time for this dialogue, as if evolution requires it to move on to the next step and for consciousness to see itself more clearly. It is the inquiry that each individual, organization, or society must engage in for its own self-awareness and realization. Who am I? Who are we together? What are we doing here? What will we create together? These are the ancient questions that traditionally have led to wisdom and appropriate solutions. My sense is that our full engagement in this process of inquiry and dialogue may allow us to uncover common denominators for a new, integrative consciousness relevant to the organizations and work of the twenty-first century.

Life, Liberty, and the Pursuit of Happiness: the Next Upgrade?

One aspect of the emerging vision of work involves an upgrade of the American dream of "life, liberty, and the pursuit of happiness"—a new iteration that recognizes the deeper meaning of each of these terms.

What actually does *life*—a truly balanced and healthy life—mean to us at this point? Can we update the nineteenth-century American Transcendentalists Emerson, Whitman, and Thoreau who envisioned integrating a healthy work ethic and enlightened consciousness, in which good work is rooted in honoring the soul? Many who apply the

Emersonian cultivation of self-mastery find that work does indeed become a vehicle for individual freedom and the realization of individual potential.

Can we upgrade the dream of *liberty* and recognize that the social-political-economic freedoms we are still seeking to implement are founded on the ultimate freedom of being awake as consciousness or spirit itself? This awakening to and recognizing of our shared universal identity offers our best hope for truly celebrating the rich diversity of our differences.

Will we continue to interpret the *pursuit of happiness* in primarily material terms, and within the confines of narrow self-interest? Or are we willing to find lasting happiness in what the wisdom traditions speak of as our true nature, that which we are and have always been? For those who do so, work ceases to be merely a means to an end and becomes the full expression of our identity, joy, and well-being.

The great challenge of these times is to awaken to the source of our doing, to realize the is-ness that underlies our busy-ness. Whether we call it soul, spirit, the sacred, God, the divine, true self, human potential, energy, consciousness, reality, or whatever else, it is the underlying essence and unifying presence within everything, the inner fount of our creativity and performance at work and in all other aspects of our lives. All sincere talk of values, integrity, love, ultimate questions, and meaning is about our relationship to this deep truth and the process by which we come to know and fully experience the source and essence of who we are.

The Great Outing

The yearning for this experience is spreading so rapidly that I liken it to an "outing," comparable to the sexual coming-out of the 1980s and early 1990s. In the 1950s, C.G. Jung observed that "the greatest taboo [of our rationalist, materialist society] is not homosexuality, it is spirituality." It's no accident that a whole generation is now coming out of the closet on this issue as well, no longer willing to keep our deepest truth locked up and separated from our work and organizations. People are waking up to the need to revitalize our workplaces and shape them in harmony with a vision of wholeness. We are witnessing a widespread awakening of consciousness that has lifted a veil and revealed a glimpse of freedom and the possibility of living and working consistent with our true nature.

I think this is what has been driving the "spirit at work" movement from the very beginning: the needs of awakening individuals to create an environment within the work setting in which their own process of awakening can flourish and expand. The call for spirituality in the workplace expresses the maturing of certain minds who are tasting the deeper consciousness, weary of the suffering of purely egoic existence, and beginning to see that work life can—indeed must—be lived and structured differently.

Advocates of human spirituality have traditionally sought to bring balm and transcendent consciousness to sick and dysfunctional environments. Now we're entering the new frontier of our corporations, in some sense major backwaters of human unconsciousness and yet also obvious opportunities for transformation. The increasing pain in so many workplaces is a subliminal demand for this healing.

But I have to admit: Despite the bright spots, I'm not seeking major change in corporations in general. I have spent most of my career teaching very specific issues, primarily focused on individuals or small groups. Only for the past few years have I been so riveted by the pain I see in the workplace that I have wanted to reach out more widely to touch it and see what can be done. Still, I am less interested in selling these ideas than to plant seeds of possibility in the fields of suffering and pray for the rain of grace.

The light and dark go together. Only through polarization can the world exist at all. Without the play of opposites, there's no manifestation. Just as yin and yang make the wheel go around, so does the onslaught of corporate mergers, restructuring, downsizing, discrimination, and harassment accompany and catalyze the explosion of spirit and wisdom at work as the healing of those conditions. The corporate upheaval is the opening for the geyser of spirit to erupt. Its deep irritants are like the sand in the oyster that generates the pearl of great wisdom and may, perhaps, evoke the compassion for dealing with it.

The essential purpose of all my work is to express the underlying union of the spiritual and the material, the ideal and the practical, the individual and the whole. I want to celebrate the marriage of heaven and earth, in which doing and being, profit and self-mastery, work and play, technology and consciousness are integrated in a seamless unity. We have the possibility now of coming to a new realization relevant to our times, an awakening to our true self and how it can be expressed in a more humane workplace that serves our material needs as well as our freedom and fulfillment in our work.

These writings integrate the three major activities and perspectives of my life, as historian, spiritual practitioner, and organizational trainer, consultant, and coach.

Chapter two on "Consciousness at Work" provides an historical and cultural overview of the expansion of consciousness in our society and the forces giving rise to greater spirituality in the workplace. It focuses on the challenges to both individual mastery and conscious organizations, and explores some of the subtle issues surrounding the language and definitions of consciousness and spirituality in the work setting.

In "Perennial Wisdom and the Workplace," I describe the non-dual or unitive approach to self-realization and how I have been translating the key principles and techniques from the world wisdom traditions into my corporate consulting.

Chapter four on "Awakening Leadership" explores the essential qualities that define leadership as a spiritual activity and opportunity to become fully conscious.

The most specific, real-time piece in the anthology is "Mark of Courageous Leadership." This chapter narrates how an individual manager I coached went through an intensive constructive feedback process and exhibited key characteristics of leadership.

Chapter six, "Tools of Mastery," describes key practices and tools I have used and taught throughout my career, with practical instruction on how you can apply them to your daily work and experience.

Finally, in "Freedom in the Flow of Work," I describe how we can experience liberation and fulfillment in our work. Here I draw directly on my personal experience of awakening, through the grace of my beloved teacher H.W.L Poonja, that dissolved the sense of separation between my work and myself, and has been the inspiration for this entire book.

II

CONSCIOUSNESS AT WORK

Awakening Consciousness in the Workplace

At work today, as Dickens said, it is the best of times and it is the worst of times. So much creative brilliance, technological innovation, boldness, and intelligence. So much stress, overwork, job insecurity, and low morale.

If most studies and polls are to be believed, many Americans are dissatisfied with their jobs and experiencing anxiety about their futures and their financial stability. The ongoing layoffs and constant reshuffling have left many people demoralized, confused, and insecure. There is anger, fear, and resentment among people who still have jobs as well as among those who have lost them. The breakdown of the "old contract"—the implicit, unwritten agreement between employer and employee that loyalty and dependence would be rewarded with promotion, security, or tenure—has further undermined loyalty and trust toward employers and heightened cynicism about company motivations. In a recent series on "The Downsizing of America" the *New York Times* described this as a "national heartache. . . . The result is the most acute job insecurity since the Depression. And this, in turn, has produced an unrelenting angst that is shattering people's notions of work and self and the very promise of tomorrow." While in 1997–98 there were promising signs of increased hiring and some improved morale, Dilbert's continued popularity seems to reflect the cynicism of many working people about the quality of life in the workplace today.

In the wake of corporate downsizing and restructuring, the current demand is for more work from fewer people. Among the survivors struggling to adjust to ongoing organizational changes and increased performance requirements, many people work harder with longer hours, spend more time in meetings, and have less time for themselves and their families. Americans work more hours and take less vacation time than any society other than Japan in the industrial world. We're seeing a rise in two- or three-income families, and increasing incidence of stress-based illness and burnout. Besides the many who have been let go, other skilled employees are choosing to leave traditional work systems to work at home, establish home businesses, and balance their lives.

These are times that force people either to draw upon their strength or cave in to hopelessness and bitterness. Transformed times are demanding transformed people.

I was talking recently with the Director of Computer Resources at a major university about how his staff is shrinking and yet being asked to do more. When asked what he expects of them, he recited an incredible litany: He wants them to be fully accountable, creative, and motivated; to be highly skilled and cross-trained; open to learning new things; willing to assume greater decision-making authority and accountability; to act with integrity and commitment; to be confident enough to take risks and not fear failure; adaptable and creative, not stuck in their job description but able to do the right thing, make immediate decisions on the spot, delight the customer, change a process, fix a problem. They should be secure enough in themselves and their competence to be entrepreneurial. They must be willing to work without a promise of permanent employment, proactively take charge of their own professional growth and career advancement, and be fully responsible for their own employability.

He and managers like him want individuals willing to express their full talents for the organization, to give themselves to the greater whole, to give up egotism for teamwork, and to surrender narrowly conceived personal ambition for the greater good. They want people who are interpersonally skillful, effective communicators, and able to work together cooperatively in self-managing teams. And on top of all that, he said, we want them to remain full of energy for longer hours and increased demands of work, and able to manage their stress so they can remain cheerful and upbeat on the job!

It became obvious that we would be asking people to change in profound ways, to rise to the occasion to be the best they can be. The demand is for higher levels of human development, perhaps even stretching us toward the next step in human evolution. We decided that what he wanted was masterful, enlightened people. Clearly, nothing less than full self-actualization would do.

Whether we consider this a fair or realistic expectation is not at issue here. It may even appear, as Dilbert shamelessly depicts, as just one more cynical management ploy to squeeze more work out of fewer people. From a larger perspective, however, I see all parties caught in a ruthless evolutionary imperative that is also an opportunity for beneficial change for individuals and their organizations.

The intense business challenges in the workplace are part of a vast historical transformation and expansion of consciousness that is taking us toward the next stage of evolution. The external forces are paired with equally powerful forces driving many individuals from within. At the same time that the workplace seems to be calling for our very souls, many of us are seeking ways to integrate our whole being more fully in our work.

We are realizing that for more than two centuries, since the beginning of the Industrial Age at least, we have had an organizational culture that emphasizes doing over being, productivity over health, and profit over ethics and meaning. We've suffered a dualistic split that divides the person into inner and outer lives and seemingly leaves the deepest self outside the workplace. The great danger now is that, as business and organizations face the relentless demand to adapt successfully to constant change, global economic competition, and technological innovation, we will continue to sacrifice our being to the survival drive.

The growing insistence on integrating spirit in the workplace arises as much from within as from without. In addition to the outward pull of a work environment demanding a profound transformation of today's work force, the push from within is coming from a growing segment of the population that is equally calling for a greater integration in the way we live and work. A significant segment of our population has reached a level of maturity and complexity that breeds higher consciousness. We are experiencing the brute force of evolution itself generating awakening for our very survival both individually and collectively.

We can identify certain general trends in this great yearning to integrate the spiritual in our everyday lives and work. In American society we have baby boomers reaching mid-life, raising children, facing sagging bodies, looking for deeper truths and values. Old hippies and longtime spiritual practitioners have come of age and into positions of prominence at work. Fundamentalists are increasingly concerned to conserve their way of life and beliefs that they see threatened and eroded by the domination of our culture by materialistic science and secular humanism. Conservative and liberal religionists alike are also expressing dissatisfaction with consumerism and the superficialities of recent decades. So many of us are yearning for a simpler way of life.

Many women have had enough of the patriarchal domination of religion and organizational life by male issues and metaphors. The deep ecology movement is integrating concern for the environment with compassion for all living beings and a mystical experience of the unity of life. For some this is the fruition of years of training and therapy in high performance and mental training techniques in athletics, or from involvement in the human potential movement based in humanistic and transpersonal psychology. All of this has cultivated an expanded view of who we are and what we are capable of accomplishing.

Many are looking beyond traditional or white Euro-centered perspectives to incorporate African, Asian, and Native American cultural forms and religious practices as well as western ethnic and pagan traditions. The Internet and World Wide Web are giving birth to emergent forms of technospirituality that blend every conceivable variety of religion, spiritual path, and consciousness discipline with new technologies of telecommunications, multimedia, and community-building in cyberspace. In the shattering of old forms there is a blending of all these influences into a new eclectic individual spirituality, based on direct personal experience.

In the intellectual realm there is an emerging synthesis of western science and ancient truths, bridging such diverse disciplines as quantum physics, chaos theory, whole systems analysis, computer and information technology, behavioral medicine, psychoneuroimmunology, and holistic health.

A new world-view is evolving with an emphasis on holism, unitive awareness, transformation, and harmony, in which even the sciences are inspiring a sense of awe and reverence for an underlying cosmic order. This new world-view is informing the nascent Integral Culture, described by Paul Ray as a fundamental spiritual, holistic, and ecological way of life of a rapidly growing socio-cultural group he calls Cultural Creatives. This group represents a transmodernism that goes beyond both traditional religions and the secular, rational-industrial modernist culture.

The growing Integral Culture is beginning to make its voice heard in the changing workplace. It comprises a significant part of a highly educated, well-trained, and self-developed population who want more power, autonomy, and creativity at work. As both the victims and the beneficiaries of the flattening of hierarchical structures, they have been given many functions previously restricted to management in order to participate more effectively in self-directed work teams, partnership and empowerment programs, and high-performance work systems. While some workers see this as a stratagem by a shrinking management to get more and better work out of fewer people, the sharing of authority and accountability with more employees also encourages greater freedom, self-motivation, and creative spirit in those ready to seize the opportunity.

It is interesting that in the United States of America's two-hundred-year experiment in implementing democracy, the corporate area is one of the least egalitarian in its structure. In many ways it resembles the old monarchical, aristocratic, hierarchical, class structures we seemingly rejected in Europe. While recent re-engineering initiatives have continued to flatten hierarchy and develop more matrixed organizations, there is still a strong dissonance between the old hierarchical legacy and a mature, self-aware, and personally responsible population coming out of a half-century of psychotherapy, consciousness-raising groups, personal growth trainings, and spiritual development. With a growing desire to have more control over their work and lives, the latter are also looking for a more equitable distribution of real power in the organization. To the extent that leadership works in partnership with this capable population, and trusts their basic instincts, abilities, and accountability, they will release the creative potential necessary to get the job done. The drive for greater freedom and control in our work is another voice of spirit speaking.

The changing demographics of American society is also promoting greater complexity and wholeness in the workplace. We are seeing a more conscious effort to accept, celebrate, and integrate the rich diversity of viewpoints, ways of thinking and doing represented in our culturally and racially diverse population. As more women and people of color enter the workplace, there is a corresponding need to free up aspects of our wholeness that are repressed in the white patriarchal system. New ways of thinking and being mean expanded consciousness at work.

All this provides the opportunity to integrate the "feminine" qualities—for example, compassion, intuition, cooperation, flexibility—with the heretofore dominant competitive, controlling, rational, "masculine" aspects of our nature. It is no accident that the concepts of "psyche" and "soul" traditionally have had a feminine character in western culture. Releasing the spirit at work requires opening the feminine mode of consciousness within the individual regardless of gender. Ironically, many women have run the danger of sacrificing their feminine qualities by adopting more masculine characteristics in order to succeed in the male-dominated workplace. For them, as for their male counterparts caught in a lifetime of macho conditioning, the challenge is to find the appropriate balance of right-brain/left-brain, or yin and yang, within them. As we do so, as individuals and as organizations, we can experience the wholeness that releases our full creative powers and frees us to be ourselves.

The convergence of these forces is at the very heart of the expansion of consciousness in the workplace. Ultimately, these trends are waves on the ocean of evolutionary momentum bringing consciousness closer to the surface as the next step in our development. What was previously a rare state of spiritual realization enjoyed by a few mystics, saints, and sages is now being tasted in various degrees by many people. Made possible in part by widespread availability of previously concealed teachers and teachings, a kind of democratization of consciousness is beginning to touch all aspects of our lives, society, and work.

The awakening is being given voice by an increasingly vocal network of leaders, consultants, and individuals at all ranks of the corporate world who are writing, speaking, and gathering in conferences and online discussions on topics such as "Soul in Business," "Profits and Prophets," "Spirit at Work," "Mindfulness in the Workplace," and "Wisdom_at_Work." A growing bibliography of passionate writings are describing how the world of business can be transformed and revitalized, how we can see our work life as sacred, and engage every action as part of our practice.

Evolutionary necessity, perhaps, but not inevitability. At this point, only a small minority of businesses are beginning to act on issues of morale, ethics, and revitalization in the workplace. As some perceptive leaders begin to suspect that their ambitious restructuring efforts may have cut out the very soul or *aliveness* of the organization, we are now seeing attempts to renew organizations, motivate people, and generate creativity—to recreate a bond of loyalty and common purpose between the company and its people.

While this movement will certainly grow, I have no illusions that all or even most of corporate America will be swept by the tide. We are slow learners, even when the pain is high. Even among those who are sympathetic with the pursuit of spiritual concerns on personal time, who admit that it may make for better people and maybe even better employees, many hold that such concerns have no place in corporate training programs, or in the workplace at all for that matter. Still, a growing segment of our population is coming to realize that effective doing comes from conscious being, and that the current restructuring of our organizations must be informed by a deeper vision that arises from our true self.

The Challenge of Mastery

This painful transition in the needs and dynamics of the work setting is challenging us to personal mastery. Because we're not accustomed to these heights and the intensity of these demands, we must learn to operate in a more rarefied altitude at a higher level of effectiveness and well-being.

We actually *need* a self-mastery that enables us to tap the deepest resources within us, take charge of our energy, go beyond our limitations, frustrations, and fears, and give our very best. The learning task before us is to attain high performance while sustaining well-being, to be productive as well as relaxed; to be proactive, vital, alive, and yet remain calm, centered, peaceful; to meet the strategic goals of the organization and also satisfy our own needs for fulfillment, enjoyment, and creative self-expression at work; to discover within the midst of chaotic change and short-term job commitments a sense of security and peace of mind.

We can only accomplish this if we recognize the benefits to us personally, and voluntarily choose the path of mastery. Without a strong stand of personal responsibility, we subtly indulge the victim mentality and remain vulnerable to being exploited. We discover our freedom when we understand that giving our best gives us ourselves.

Indeed, perhaps the greatest incentive to mastery is the collapse of the "old contract" in the workplace. The breakdown of this traditional co-dependent syndrome is a tremendous force pushing workers to become empowered, to look to themselves for identity, motivation, and success. It's driving people to find the source of inspiration within themselves, not in the company; to discover their security within themselves, not in job tenure; to find freedom in taking charge of their own well-being, and in their choice to be present and committed in their work. The erosion of the old way is a wake-up call, just as drug addiction and domestic violence are wake-up calls, to forge a new way that works.

How many will hear the alarm and get out of their slumber? How many will succumb to despair, cynicism, resentment, blame? Freedom and awakened consciousness do not come cheaply. In some sense, as the old spiritual traditions pointed out, you must give up everything to be free. "Freedom's just another word for nothing left to lose," sang Saint Janis. More and more people are realizing how precariously close they are to nothing left to lose.

We must discover what Alan Watts called "the wisdom of insecurity." This is a security deeper than the physical and material. It must be found within ourselves, in the intangible world of being. Once we really get it that there is ultimately no such thing as job security, that we're all temps in a situation of unpredictable transience whether we have jobs or not, we may see that our very survival requires realizing our deepest essence and wholeness. Nothing else will do. Times of trial and suffering bring forth the purest transformations.

It's no accident that this challenge also comes at a time when the whole context of spiritual life is also changing. In the past, people have felt a need to get away to supportive environments—monasteries, ashrams, hermitages, the desert, the forest, retreat centers—to realize the Self. And while retreat will certainly remain a crucial support for awakening consciousness, we are now saying that you can do it at work. You *can* do it in the midst of the pressures for high performance, creativity, responsibility, and business success—an arena which, until now at least, has offered very little acceptance or support for such a quest.

The challenge isn't for the weak-willed. It calls for an extraordinarily strong individual stand: the courage and commitment of Spartacus, as John Renesch reminds us. As the great Chinese Zen Master Ta Hui said to his monks who begged him to let them stay in their protected monastery when he forcibly evicted them and sent them out into the world to deal with the everyday realities of family and work: "Anyone can hold a sleeping baby."

Most of us find spirituality more comfortable in protective, benign settings. Living the conscious life has never been easy. Yet at a certain point we come to recognize that hostile, unsupportive settings are the burning fire in which our mastery and determination are tempered. Nothing substitutes for that experience. A more grounded and integrated consciousness for the twenty-first century may well be forged in the white-hot crucible of the modern workplace—if, as we shall explore later, we are collectively willing to consider what kind of work culture and processes will best support this individual transformation.

For the work force, the central challenge here is to view work as more than just a job, that is, to see one's "profession" as a place of personal and spiritual development. This shift is entirely in keeping with the original meaning and some common associations we have with these words. In our vernacular, we may refer to work as our "profession," a term that for medieval Europeans meant a declaration of faith—to profess or take vows as a member of a religious community. The earliest "corporations" were literally spiritual bodies, associated with the Church, of artisans or tradespeople with distinct rights and religious functions. Or we may refer to work as our "vocation," which also referred originally to an inner calling or divine summons to live out your life's purpose. Another powerful use of the word work is in referring to one's spiritual practice, *sadhana* in the Hindu sense, or "working on yourself" in the transformational disciplines.

The potential of mastery here is for truly fulfilling oneself at work. It involves the commitment to working on ourselves and promoting our personal, spiritual, and professional growth in the work context. It means seeing in the mandate to meet the organization's needs the opportunity for creative self-expression of our potential.

Realistically, I expect only a small minority of people to see their work as spiritual practice and an opportunity for mastery. For others, their well-being may be served best by leaving the workplace or radically redefining what they do for a living. It is likely that the majority of people in the work force will continue to be caught in the struggle for survival, and that they will make their subliminal deals for material success and security with a capricious work system that chews up people as quickly as it shifts business strategies.

For those who choose it, mastery calls for a heightened self-awareness of who we are and what we are capable of. It is a discipline of living by principles and skillfully applying tools that can balance two fundamental needs that converge in the workplace: the need to make a living and the need to fulfill ourselves. In so doing we may be able to create work and organizations that better reflect our dreams and commitments, our energy and talents.

Indeed, as individuals become more conscious, the possibility of conscious organizations is arising.

Conscious Organizations

We now have the opportunity to create a mutually beneficial integration in the work setting—a fit between organizations' needs for a high-performing, motivated work force and individuals' needs for well-being, fulfillment, and meaning in their work. Businesses and organizations today are facing the tremendous challenge to create appropriately resilient forms and structures that can adapt successfully to constantly changing conditions. Moving to the next step in organizational evolution requires tapping the full intelligence, talent, energy, and creativity of the individuals who comprise the organization. What it takes for adaptive organizations to emerge is simultaneously an opportunity for individuals to realize their full potential at work. Organizational success and individual self-actualization can go hand in hand.

This calls for a new understanding between leadership and employees on the meaning and purpose of work that would benefit both corporate strategy and individual fulfillment. It is time for leadership to recognize that the individual spirit is the true source of business revitalization and success, and accordingly, to commit the resources and provide the encouraging environment to unleash that creative energy fully. We can no longer repress the human spirit at work and leave at home or in the parking lot the source of high performance and success.

If employers cannot promise lifetime tenure and job security, they *can* provide an empowering environment and opportunities for personal, spiritual, and professional growth. This commitment is key to making the shift from paternalistic control-dependency organizations to streamlined, empowered organizations of self-motivated, entrepreneurial people who know their own worth and demonstrate it in their work.

The situation calls for enlightened stewardship that understands it is in the best interests of organizations to promote the freedom, satisfaction, and well-being of their people, that if they want real high performance they must directly address the attitudes, motivation, and inner life of the work force.

In return for employees working on themselves and giving their best performance to the organization, a conscious organization provides them opportunities to nurture themselves and enhance their self-mastery. There are many corporate initiatives being adopted today that sketch out essential components of the awakening organization. The recent emphasis on " the learning organization" or "high-performance work systems" has generated strong commitment to the continuous learning and improvement of individuals and the organization. The conscious organization creates an atmosphere that celebrates the diversity of approaches and work styles of all its people. It values the individual and encourages and rewards each person's creativity, innovativeness, and risk-taking. It provides the education, training, performance reviews, coaching and mentoring essential to promoting personal and professional development. There is an understanding that skillful interpersonal relationships and open communication, including the free flow of constructive and positive feedback, not only enhance business performance and teamwork but generate intangible morale as well.

The conscious organization demonstrates a commitment to the health and well-being of all employees, reflected in wellness and stress management programs, stringent safety precautions, and a clean, light environment. We are seeing a more open attitude toward flex time, day care options, and other ways to balance work and family, plus a growing awareness of the creative value and healthiness of fun, humor, and play in the workplace. Meditation and music rooms for quiet reflection are beginning to show up in the rectilinear halls of corporate America, and even the faint resonance of prayer or drumming circles may now be heard in state-of-the-art, high-tech conference rooms. Ethical concerns are reflected in conscious choices about contributing to the local community and allowing time for employees to do volunteer work, as well as developing ecologically sound products and processes, and cleaning up and protecting the local environment. Ultimately, a conscious organization aligns its corporate policies and actions with long-term planetary evolution and the well-being of the whole earth.

Leadership's willingness to support this transformation is the fundamental key to the success of conscious organizations. Those leaders bold and caring enough to take the stand may come to realize the essentially spiritual nature of leadership, and that their compassionate concern for the well-being of their employees bears deep healing benefits for themselves as well as for achievement at work.

This new contract is essential if we are to resolve the inherent contradiction in many of our workplaces today of trying to get more, better, and faster work out of fewer people. Without this, the result for many is simply more stress, longer hours, less leisure and family time, increased frustration and cynicism. We cannot have optimal productivity without inner peace. Without attending to our being, our doing may very well kill us.

This commitment to our own well-being is our major safeguard against getting sucked in to the endless demands for continuous improvement and still higher performance. It is up to each of us to determine what is do-able within the self-defined boundaries of our own health and happiness. In the same way, we can only avoid participating in, or being subjected to, unethical or exploitative business practices when we are willing to be grounded in our own truth and self-knowledge, and take the risks of living and speaking with integrity in our work. This home base will empower people to participate authentically and creatively in the corporate vision and make their real contribution to their work.

We are finally coming to recognize the existence of two equally valid, mutually interdependent bottom lines: business profit and individual well-being, organizational success and personal transformation. It will be fascinating to see if the convergence of work and spirit will give birth to a new, integrated bottom line as the foundation for a truly conscious organization.

The very thrust of evolution is creating the opportunity for this union, promising greater wholeness and awareness for individuals and organizations alike. It is as if consciousness is lifting a veil and allowing us to glimpse the deeper ground of being where all doing comes from. By fully exploring this glimpse, we may come to see that it is actually possible for organizations to become conscious in the same way that individuals can be self-aware, and that organizations can act self-referentially as individuals can. Of course, collective awareness is a much more complex and rare phenomenon than individual awareness. Yet the current efforts toward community building, learning organizations, and Bohmian dialogue are creating the link between individual and collective consciousness. In essence, organizations are simply people, people relating in certain structures and patterns. A conscious organization is the synergy of the personal awareness and transformations of the individuals involved.

The rapid spread of computers, information technology, and telecommunications is a powerful integrating and liberating force laying the infrastructure for the conscious organization. Greater access to information and the personal computer make possible the empowerment of individuals and the flattening of hierarchy. The new intranets, groupware, and networking capabilities promise to strengthen interdependent collaboration within teams and organizations as a context for a shared mind to emerge at work. The emerging web of relationships increasingly reflects the underlying unity and interdependence of existence.

Computers and information technology are clear indications of growing complexity and consciousness in organizations. They represent a rapidly proliferating nervous system needed to store and circulate corporate intelligence. Within the organization, awareness is a function of the flow of information, which is literally consciousness "in-form." Accessible information—not "data" alone, but ideas, feelings, visions, feedback, decisions, policies, dialogues, the whole range of human self-expression—freely flowing through open communication provides the self-correcting intelligence required for the successful learning organization to adapt rapidly to internal and external challenges. Effective communication systems allow the shared reservoir of knowledge and experience at work to circulate as a collective consciousness. Information is literally the aliveness and creativity that taps the group potential and allows organizations to self-organize to more mature structures.

The emergence of something we might call a "collective mind" can come from this expanded ability—both technological and personal—to communicate and relate together with clarity, openness, and integrity. This process can create the common organizational visions, values, and processes that generate a shared consciousness, or energy field, within which the harmonious flow of high performance can occur. As consciousness expands, organizations, like individuals, can merge their self-interest with that of the greater whole. In so doing, conscious organizations, like awakened individuals, can have a naturally appropriate relationship of authentic service with the larger environment.

What we need most of all is a way of living and working that offers real solutions to the do-more-with-less, do-less-with-less, do-more-with-more conundrum. This is a dilemma that can't be fully resolved by daytimers, working smarter, better computers, more bandwidth, elaborate networking, or even thirty-hour work weeks per se.

Ultimately, it involves an integrated way of being and doing known as "flow." Chinese Taoists call it *wei wu wei,* active non-action. Zen refers to it as a state of effortless effort. In the Indian tradition of non-dual awakening, it is called spontaneous appropriate action.

The flow state is actually quite ordinary, and occurs for most people every day in moments of full absorption that usually pass unnoticed. It is really a natural condition, and perhaps we scare people off or make it sound inaccessible when we tout it as an exalted or extraordinary state. It is revealed when we're willing to be mindful of what is, to be fully present, inwardly quiet, and absorbed in our work.

In the here-now moment of no-thought, the sense of separation falls away. Even the restraints of mind-created time can be transcended, and the individual becomes an open receptivity through which the ever present being-awareness-energy flows. The bodymind is intuitively moved to harmonious responsiveness with the wider whole. It attains a natural effectiveness that is part of the implicit order and has been described by great sages and high performers throughout the centuries (including recent 49er quarterbacks!). Here is a state of vital spontaneity in which appropriate action and effective work can occur, in which the individual is drawing on the resourcefulness of the totality itself, and where the intellect and senses are fully functional. There is a nonconceptual knowing of the whole that sees clearly what is to be done. In this flow our inherent potential and creativity are released and we can make our full contribution in our work and to one another.

Where Angels Fear to Tread

The discussion of wisdom and spirituality in the workplace is fraught with traps and pitfalls. It activates people's fears of being proselytized, hoodwinked, or cultified, and of having their privacy invaded. If one is to address these issues at all, it must emerge organically, through day-to-day practice and application, from the mature fruition of wisdom and experience. It is even more important that it come about, not from an impulse to teach, preach, or proselytize, but as a natural flowering of a compassionate desire to serve the unfolding of others.

The big danger nowadays is that people with little experience will jump in and get "trained" to facilitate this, as if it were an academic subject matter or simple skills course. It is certainly not a training. Frankly, after studying and practicing for some thirty years, I have only begun to feel comfortable addressing these matters face to face in the workplace.

We have to realize that this dialogue takes place in the context of deep and passionately held differences of belief and spiritual perspective in our society. It is important to engage the dynamics of the process with your eyes wide open and with as few illusions as possible.

This incipient conversation is an aspect of the ongoing experiment with diversity that our society has not yet resolved. Finding a common ground for people of different races, classes, genders, sexual orientations, and ways of thinking has been warming us up to face the increasingly vocal differences in spiritual traditions. Many groups claim truth is on their side, claims often associated with intense dogmatism, violence, and oppression in the most brutal chapters of human history.

The whole issue is inherently difficult to discuss because, in my view, authentic spirituality—as distinct from religion—is an intensely private relationship to the basic indescribable mystery. It then shows up through a multitude of unique experiences, many languages, and various social agendas all operating simultaneously.

Resistance to discussing spirituality in the work setting takes many forms. It may come from people basically not interested in the inner life or its appropriateness to work, or from religious people who feel it's best to keep spiritual matters (as they define them) out of work, similar to keeping it out of schools or government.

Then there are those who favor spirituality at work, but want only their way to be represented. These people may take a dogmatic and argumentative stand toward other approaches. With many of them, there is very little room for discussion when the language has spiritual connotations of any real depth. If the conversation is framed in some other way—focused on consciousness or wisdom rather than "spirituality," for example, or in scientific, health-oriented, or human potential concepts—then it may be easier to move toward an understanding.

Our society seems to have entered a period perhaps similar in intensity to the Crusades, in which fundamentally opposing spiritual views lock horns. I am committed to finding a common ground of understanding for this difficult issue that is unitive and inclusive. Unfortunately that very position is seen by some as a deep falsehood itself, a deception leading people into error or worse. People who are dogmatic about their religion tend to see any genuinely open discussion of spirituality as a threat.

Instead of setting people against one another as partisan combatants, we need to understand better how pairs of opposites generate, sustain, and need one another. At first glance, the process of polarization looks as if people are taking extreme positions at opposite ends of the spectrum. Each end may represent a legitimate value, but one that must also be balanced with its opposite value in order to exist at all. Polarization represents a kind of balance that is unstable and conflictual, symptoms of the failure to bring together those views that are in tension.

If we look deeper, the polarizations likely to arise in discussions of spirituality are expressions of the inherent dualism of the mind, which by its very nature divides the unity of existence into pairs. It divides the one existence into perceiving subject and perceived object, you and me, right and wrong, yes and no, and so on. Once this basic dualism is established, the law of opposites works inexorably. "Yes" needs "no" for its existence. Without its opposite it has no meaning or substance. A sense of righteousness needs evil to fight and witches to hunt. Throughout history "good" people have projected out their own repressed tendencies and objectified them as the "other," with whom they engaged in conflict as a form of self-justification.

I see no full resolution or integration until there is some realization of how dualism works to mask the inherent underlying unity and create the suffering of separation. The unitive vision offers a context large enough to embrace the apparent opposites, so that opposites can perceive themselves as part of a larger unity or, we could say, recognize themselves in one another. In this true self-recognition a natural reconciliation can occur.

As my colleague Andrew Bard Schmookler wisely commented: "The idea that the truth lies between the extremes would be the cliché it appears to be if it meant only the need for a mechanical compromise, a splitting of the difference. But the real truth lies not between but above the extremes. The great spiritual leaders of humankind—a Buddha or a Jesus or a Gandhi or a Saint Francis or a Dalai Lama—are people who have integrated values that seem to be in tension into a form that isn't just a compromise on a lowest common denominator. At their level of integration, one might be at once freer than the libertines and more disciplined than the straight-laced. One might be both a better warrior than the hawks and a better peacemaker than the doves."

These great leaders have known first-hand the unity of existence— not so much as an intellectual concept, but as their very being itself. What is striking is that they have embodied qualities that reflect uni- tive consciousness: openness, humility, compassion, love, gentleness, acceptance. These are the truly integrative qualities. To the extent that we allow ourselves to embody these qualities we can become expres- sions of, and agents for, the unitive solution. This is not meant as a well-articulated conceptual position, but rather a way of being that can embrace the polarities and hold everything and everyone in its huge heart.

The Language of Mystery

In my work with corporations since the early 1980s, these topics have emerged spontaneously as a natural consequence of exploring issues of empowerment, stress and change management, team-building, lead- ership, and globalization. As the conversations deepened, more subtle aspects of consciousness became relevant. The most crucial task be- came to cultivate a language adequate to the inquiry. My most creative challenge has been translating between the languages of consciousness and work, and finding terms that touch our true being.

I've come to understand, however, that we just aren't going to have all people feel included with any single set of words. There are simply too many different perspectives out there, and different doorways for everyone. Each person has a certain authentic voice and language that truly expresses their real experience. We do our best by being as open as we can, respecting the plurality of views and making room for differ- ences. There are folks out there who will resonate to you. Others won't.

I've been fermenting with this question of language for years. I have used different languages in my career, intuitively seeking what language will work best for a given audience. Over the years I have learned to speak the language of Buddhism with Buddhists, Hinduism with Hindus, Judaeo-Christianity with the peoples of the Old and New Testaments, and the language of science and whole systems in a more secular dialogue. While each language is appropriate in its context, they are specific cultural expressions of the deeper, unspeakable truth at the core of the Perennial Philosophy. In the long run, there is still the question of what language best expresses my version of this universal experience.

Words like "spirituality," "religion," "soul," or "God" are a minor part of my vocabulary. They have so many connotations to get through and some very heavy baggage for many people. Even though from time to time I use them as *lingua franca*, I prefer to focus people freshly on their direct, inner experience and how they can express that with as little baggage as possible.

I emphasize words like consciousness, wisdom and self-awareness, true nature or true self, energy, power, freedom, compassion, detachment. This language works for me both philosophically and psychologically. Some of it also has a greater basis in science. I sometimes use "spirit" as a substitute or shorthand for consciousness or energy, and "soul" as the deepest reservoir of individual potential or the individualized expression of the one true Self.

The real challenge is knowing what you mean to say and then selecting words that best express that. My cautionary note to people trying to discuss spirituality is that they clarify and speak from their own direct experience. There needs to be a deepening and maturing of one's own self-awareness for the appropriate language to emerge. Otherwise we just have more of the blind leading the blind. My language has been changing as the realization unfolds, and I expect further evolution of my language in the ongoing expansion of consciousness.

I'd say the key to real understanding is to establish intimate relationship with people, lay the groundwork for honest dialogue, talk about openness, problems of translation, and the sharing of experience. With this as a basis, we can raise the question of language itself and discuss it openly.

I've also discovered that we have to balance our concern for the "right" language with an understanding that the work goes on subliminally anyway beneath the conceptual level. It is your being—that is, your own consciousness and love—that really touches people, regardless of what you're saying. It is this underlying being that is always, already, in communion with itself.

Ultimately, we can hold the language issue lightly by remembering that we're discussing mystery itself, an ineffable personal experience that is beyond mind to understand and language to describe. Silence, the source of all sound and thought, is the perfect expression of what can't be said. In classical Indian music, the spaces between the notes are more important than the notes themselves. In the silent spaces between the words, people with very different beliefs and approaches can discover their true commonality and communion.

Spirituality & Religion

A natural outgrowth of developing effective language is to clarify what we're really trying to discuss. For starters, we need to distinguish the force of pure spirituality from the particular forms it may be taking. While I am presenting my own interpretations here, I intend to provide as inclusive and unitive an approach as possible. Because spirituality is so uniquely personal to each individual, we need to find a framework that allows for an open dialogue in which our differences can enrich our understanding and support each of us to manifest our true nature at work.

Historical context is crucial for the language, metaphors, and nuance with which people express the wisdom of their deep realizations. It might even be that historical contexts shape the kind of spiritual experience people have. There may be no way of knowing if what we describe today is really the same as what historical saints and sages have told us. We may in fact be developing a new expression of consciousness that is truly relevant to the needs of our time.

By any name, spirituality is a quality inherent in all human beings. It is the process by which we come to know and realize our True Self or Source Reality.

It is expressed in a way of living that is characterized by compassionate speech and action consistent with our deepest truth. The fundamental litmus test of spirituality is our integrity, a loving, harmonious way of being and doing in which we walk our talk. True spirituality speaks for itself. As Mahatma Gandhi gently responded when asked by a reporter what his message was: "My life is my message."

Spirituality is the mysterious and inexplicable essence at the heart of religion. Religion is the way we seek to explain, codify, preserve, and extend our spiritual experience. Spirituality is the source of religion but not restricted to it. It is a direct, personal reality which need not be mediated by a priesthood, church, or ritual, and can be experienced by anyone regardless of religious affiliation.

Spirit is the vital force that enlivens not only religion, but also art, music, dance, literature, science, the entire world of creativity. Religion traditionally arises as the formal expression of spiritual realization or unitive consciousness—usually centered on the awakening of the founder and a few sages and mystics. It develops the beliefs, rituals, and practices by which others can also have that realization (*re-ligio:* relink to the Source).

Religion goes through historical cycles in which it may lose its vitality and relevance, and fossilize into institutionalized doctrines and rituals which no longer express the inner spirituality it claims. Traditionally, religions go through periods of renewal when the essential spirituality erupts to revitalize and purify the cultural forms—as we are seeing in the current awakening in our society today.

Whereas religion is historical and changing, spirit is timeless and unchanging. Religion is cultural, sometimes associated with a unique ethnic or social group, while spirit is the universal essence in everyone that transcends all differences.

Religion offers explanations, meaning, purpose, a mythology and context for life. Spirituality embraces the fundamental mystery that is beyond language, concept, and ordinary sense perceptions. Spirit is known and experienced on its own terms. Whereas religion tends to emphasize morality, ethics, and rules for behavior, spirit is non-conceptual, non-judgmental, and unconditional, generating action that is free, spontaneous, and appropriate to the well-being of the whole.

It would be fascinating to work out how different approaches—eastern and western, unitive and dualistic spiritualities—have different implications and relevance to the work setting. Do different realizations guide us toward certain understandings and applications at work? Can we find a synthesis that truly integrates for a universal applicability? Or is that just unrealistic wishful thinking or homogenizing the beautiful diversity to some bland least common denominator that would be basically unsatisfying?

The Isness of Business

Ultimately, what we call spirit is who and what we really are. It is the being at the source of all doing, the unchanging is-ness abiding within our constantly moving busy-ness. This underlying conscious essence is always present, wherever we are. The great challenge of these times is not merely to awaken to the true self, but to do so right in the midst of our work.

We find our being when we turn within to face ourself. The powerful mandates of organizational change and survival are prompting us to open a self-aware conversation in the work setting in which we turn within to explore individual and organizational identity, vision, purpose, character, competencies, and resources. It is this deep self-reflection, both personal and organizational, that can empower us to change successfully and release our potential for effective, appropriate action.

The inward-turning questions for both individuals and organizations are basically similar. Who are we, What is our identity, What are our resources and strengths? What do we stand for, What are our values and commitments? What are we doing here, Where are we going, What do we want to create together? Out of this inquiry we shape the vision, mission, values, and structure of the organization.

As specific individuals, we can ask: Is my job a place where I can fulfill my potential, express my talents, energy, and creativity in ways that are satisfying to me? Can work be true self-expression or am I withholding too much of myself here? Is work a place where I can have consistency between my values and my behavior? Can I live out my integrity or right livelihood here? What is the meaning of my work in the context of my deepest purpose and commitments? Can I see work as service or contribution to something deeper or higher than just my individual self-interest? Can my work be spiritual practice, a place to be self-aware, conscious, meditative, prayerful, giving, compassionate, loving?

As a conscious organization, we can ask: Are we committed to promoting ongoing learning and continuous improvement that supports both the individual and the organization? Are we willing to create an atmosphere that values the individual, celebrates diversity and authenticity? Will we cultivate interpersonal harmony, love, compassion, and acceptance for one another? Do we see the value of encouraging inner peace, patience, and humility? Can we permit joy, fun, humor, and play as essential to creative work? Are we willing to serve and support one another, and work together collaboratively? Will we participate in honest, open, respectful communication that generates an atmosphere of trust and integrity, and give one another feedback and recognition that inspires and brings out the best in one another? Are we committed to the well-being of the whole, and to creating the right balance between work, family, and our inner life?

The tools of this self-awareness are inquiry and dialogue. We ground our inquiry in relaxation, centering, and meditative introspection that open us to the quietness of our being. In that silence we find peace, access intuitive knowing, and revitalize our creative energy. Having gone deep within, we can expand out through dialogue to share our discoveries with one another.

A crucial key to successful dialogue is listening. Listening deeply to yourself and others, being fully present and attentive, is an essential spiritual practice at work today which opens us to the deeper wisdom within us all. If we are courageous enough to face ourselves and one another, our personal wisdom can become the collective intelligence, a common reservoir of knowledge and experience that can enliven the organization. Through this inquiry and dialogue, the shared individual spirit can become the resilient collective soul of the organization.

As a consultant, I've come to realize that the most I can offer is simply encouragement and a little expertise to allow organizations to give birth to themselves. More and more, I live with the trust that a perfectly organic and appropriate form can emerge for each organization if its people are willing to go through a kind of natural childbirth. Like midwives, we don't really do it for them. We simply allow their natural form to emerge from their own ingredients, resources, people. We are attendants to a self-organizing process that is enacting itself through us. The less I do the better. At best I create a space in which they can discover themselves.

Consciousness: A Global Perspective

To fully understand the expansion of consciousness in the workplace, we must take a global perspective on the rapidly converging forces of business globalization, global telecommunications, and computer technology. Taken together, for better or for worse, they are creating a planetary network that is laying the infrastructure for a possible global unitive consciousness.

From the whole systems perspective, we see that evolution allows for the emergence of higher orders of consciousness as living systems attain greater complexity in their adaptation to evolutionary imperatives. Systems thinking may be materialist-based: i.e., awareness emerges from matter at a certain level of complexity. Or it may be more idealist, as described by Hegel or Sri Aurobindo, who saw consciousness or spirit revealing itself through matter as its vehicle. To grasp its full significance, it is important to see globalization as a visible manifestation of this unifying consciousness. Looking at the ramifying global technological-economic network as an evolving self-organizing system, we can see it generating a wider consciousness to embrace greater cultural diversity, social and economic complexity, and technological connectivity within an emerging global organism.

When historians look back on the last half of the twentieth century, it's likely they will highlight business globalization as a major force in the transformation of the planet. We can see it as the culmination of a five-hundred-year cycle of world history that began with European commercial expansion overseas in the fifteenth and sixteenth centuries and progressed through colonialism and imperialism to extend western technological-economic hegemony over much of the world. The current move toward corporate globalization and the accelerating expansion of the Internet and the World Wide Web are the closing of this circle.

The globalization process is driven by the same constellation of motives that launched the western expansion in the first place: what in the Renaissance was quaintly described as the quest for "Gold, God, and Glory." By "gold" we mean, of course, the drive for economic survival, profit, and control of markets, conditioned by the intense competitiveness of capitalism that pits individual against individual, company against company, and one national economy against another. Globalization is clearly impelled by the maturing realization that it is crucial to the success of larger corporate players, and by the recognition of many businesses that unless they participate in the global economy they risk stagnation or extinction.

What distinguishes globalization from the imperialism of earlier historical eras, however, is the increasing reality of global interdependence. It is becoming obvious that we are all mutually reliant aspects of a vast intertwined system of global economics in which our self-interest is now intimately bound together with the fate of our neighbors. The sense of mutual interdependence, while it arises from the sheer need for economic survival, may well be the self-adapting corrective to the traditional competitiveness that has previously moved the world market. While competition will doubtless continue, the context is increasingly one of collaboration and partnership. In the long run we are all in the same boat, and recognizing our unity and acting in supportive ways ultimately serves the interest of the whole. Our concern for the plight of other countries and our willingness to help bail them out of economic hot water is a direct reflection of this dawning common self-interest. It is increasingly obvious that in an interdependent world, national self-interest ultimately becomes one with the self-interest of the whole, which may then become the realistic basis for genuine compassion that serves the good of all.

But the challenges are daunting: How to deal with a multinational, ethnically and linguistically diverse work force with differing values and ways of working, spread out in offices, plants, and labs around the globe; how to develop organizational structures that balance centralization and local autonomy, with sufficient uniformity of structure, norms, and procedures to assure consistent quality and performance; and how to find the optimal connectivity for the most effective flow of people, ideas, technology, and products around the globe?

For most American companies doing business overseas, globalization is a buzz word meaning little more than "increased international presence." Yet as they expand their international activities and have sustained intimate contact and direct business dealings with peoples of different cultures, it becomes obvious that true globalization will mean relating more responsively and effectively with a growing diversity of foreign cultures and societies. It literally means that westerners will need to expand their cultural awareness and be increasingly flexible and skillful in the way they interact and do business with their global partners, colleagues, customers, and employees. If we are to make the global network work, East and West, Americans and Europeans, even the specific Asian cultures among themselves, will need to come to a greater understanding and appreciation of the different ways of doing and being.

This is probably the most sustained challenge humanity has yet faced to find a place from which we can truly understand, value, and benefit from our cultural differences. Embracing global diversity means accepting and appreciating our various cultural, ethnic, racial, and religious perspectives. Cross-cultural understanding could lay the groundwork for an awareness of human commonality and unity. It ultimately challenges each of us to tap the depths of our own being that knows multiplicity to be expressive of its own underlying unity.

While the process is so far being accomplished within a primarily western cultural and technological context, western sensitivity to global diversity issues must eventually involve an attempt to incorporate appropriate elements of other world cultures. The West, at this point, is winning the game of global cultural hegemony—our languages, technologies, ways of doing business, and organizational structures form the basic template for the globalization process. Yet to be fully successful in the long run, the western context needs to be enriched by each culture's ways.

It is time for the West, especially Americans, to go beyond parochialism, ethnocentrism, and traditional stereotypes to understand and learn from other cultures. Continuous improvement and competitive benchmarking on a global scale mean expanding our cultural context to include what works, not just what we are accustomed to within our national or cultural "style." Here it is important to include these ingredients in a rich, flavorful, global stew, not some bland homogenized puree.

The nervous sytem for an emerging global consciousness is being laid by the dazzling innovations of computer and information technology, and the accelerating proliferation of global telecommunications, the Internet and World Wide Web. Cyberspace is a new domain for sharing our underlying unity of consciousness or spirit. In the past, communities were shaped and defined by culture, race, language, geography. Now we are seeing nascent global communities brought together by consciousness—shared interests, visions, beliefs, passions—carried through the ganglia of electronic media, a kind of macro parallel to the way intelligent communication flows through the psycho-neuroimmunologic channels of the human mindbody organism. The global network is transcending time and space, bringing many people together in the possibility of new, more subtle ways of relating. What we are actually dealing with here is consciousness riding lasers of light, pulsing through an expanding lattice of optical fiber for nearly instantaneous communication with itself.

This global consciousness was foreseen by Father Pierre Teilhard de Chardin, the French Jesuit philosopher, mystic, and paleontologist. In *The Phenomenon of Man* (1955) Teilhard prophesied the emergence of the "noosphere," literally an aura of expanded human intelligence and light that would encircle the globe. Peter Russell later termed this nascent planetary consciousness the "global brain" in his book of that title. The earth, like human beings and organizations, is in a process that Barbara Marx Hubbard calls conscious evolution. Deep ecologists have named this self-regulating conscious planetary organism after the ancient Greek earth Goddess, Gaia, who may be developing a tellurian halo.

The economic and technological forces moving humanity toward unitive consciousness are surface waves arising from the depths of the inner drive to self-realization. The same power calling individuals to awaken to our true nature as being-consciousness is operating in our organizations and other domains of our life as well. The conscious individual, the conscious organization, and the conscious planet are all movements of the universal consciousness, the one Self of all whose reflection is now being revealed to those with eyes to see. Here we have microcosm and macrocosm, individuals and their organizations, being offered the opportunity of a new wisdom, identity and wholeness. The principles and tools needed to embark on such an adventure have been developing in the wisdom traditions for centuries.

III

PERENNIAL WISDOM
AND THE WORKPLACE

The Perennial Wisdom

At the heart of the great world cultures lies the quest for knowledge, truth, and the ultimate fulfillment of human life. The wisdom path has sought to integrate intellect and experience, insight and action, for a harmonious and effective way of being in daily life. As we explore the various meanings of wisdom, we embark on a journey to the depths of reality and our true nature.

In one sense wisdom is knowledge embodied, come to fruition in the integrity of our speech and actions. We are wise when we have digested the accumulated learning of our life experience. This culminates in clear seeing into reality and the nature of things. Wisdom is a penetrating insight into yourself and people, an understanding of how things work, of basic principles of nature, of the cause and effect of the universe. It is seeing life for what it is, not being deceived by appearances. It is living without illusions. Our wisdom gives us the ability to act effectively, to know intuitively when and how to respond appropriately to what occurs in a way that supports the well-being of others.

In another sense, wisdom is knowing how little you know. Ignorance is the beginning of wisdom, Socrates cautioned us. Zen practitioners call it "beginner's mind," which is truly open and fresh, willing to remain innocent and receptive to life, not attached to our knowledge. It is the willingness to be empty, and thus open to learning and growing. This is the source of creativity and innovation, the key to continuous improvement, and the essential personal ingredient in the learning organization.

Wisdom, then, is an open-ended process of ongoing learning and growth. Ever expanding into the unknown, there is no end to its depth. Ironically, the current explosion of information technology has opened us to the virtual infinity of knowledge available and the impossibility of any one individual actually mastering it all. Thus, expanding knowledge means expanding ignorance, which cultivates the fertile ground of humility in which deeper wisdom can sprout.

Knowing that you don't know is a receptivity to a deeper knowing. Ultimately I experience wisdom born in wonder and awe, in the ability to appreciate the fundamental mystery of the universe and to hold lightly the relative and changing beliefs, theories, models, explanations we use to guide us through life. It sees through the filter of interpretation to that which cannot be described or explained. This is a meta-knowingness, a context rather than specific content, which views the enigma of life as a reality to be enjoyed rather than a problem to be solved. Here knowing and unknowing are one and the same.

More specifically I am referring to a grand tradition of deep knowing that has come to be known as the Perennial Philosophy. It is not a single, systematic teaching, but rather a confluence of currents found in many world religious, philosophical, and psychological traditions. The perennial wisdom expresses a commonality of experience and perspective cutting across geography, cultures, disciplines, found in both western and eastern, spiritual and secular, scientific and contemplative, experimental and experiential approaches. It provides a broad, cross-cultural framework of understanding and practical tools for people engaged in awakening in the workplace.

The Perennial Philosophy declares that there is a single truth, an indivisible reality which is the essence of life and the core of every human being. It is founded on the direct realization of our true nature or ultimate reality here and now. While this awakening is beyond mind to grasp or language to describe, we attempt to convey the ineffable experience with words like freedom, wisdom, love, enlightenment, bliss, peace, eternal life. Whatever we call it, it is the fully experienceable ultimate state of human fulfillment, an awakening to our identity with the unitive presence which is the underlying source of everything. This supreme mystery has been given many names: Consciousness, Spirit, Absolute, Self, Buddha, God, Being, Reality, Tao, Energy, Truth. The non-dual—or unitive—realization at the heart of the Perennial Philosophy is the direct knowing that you are That, and that all phenomena and beings are manifestations of this-that-you-are which lives in and as each of us. Life is the opportunity to know this fully and to express it lovingly and joyfully in our lives and work.

Many traditions have touched this truth and seek to express it in terms consistent with their own historical, cultural, and philosophical orientation. It has been expressed by the mystics of the world's religions as well as by quantum physicists, holistic health practitioners, deep ecologists, whole systems theorists, and organizational development specialists. It is as American as Emerson and Whitman, as mysterious and paradoxical as the great Chinese Zen Master Huang Po, as lofty and divine as the medieval Christian Meister Eckhart. It is revealed in the prophetic speeches of the Native American Chief Seattle, the ecstatic love poetry of the Sufi mystic poet Rumi, and the esoteric learning of the Jewish Kabbalists and joyful celebrations of Israel Baal Shem and the Hasidim. Rarely expressed as a systematic philosophy, it describes a way of seeing and being in the world that arises from the direct personal experience of fulfillment and unity with life.

Recent interpreters of this wisdom have been Aldous Huxley, Alan Watts, Paul Brunton, Abraham Maslow, Fritjof Capra, Copthorne MacDonald, Margaret Wheatley, Peter Russell, and—in my view our most lucid, comprehensive proponent—Ken Wilber. These "gnostic intermediaries" as Roger Walsh has called them, are carrying forward this rich global heritage as the basis for a new transformative culture which incorporates the perennial wisdom in our day-to-day lives and work.

Applying the Wisdom Path at Work

The unitive realization is the inspiration and background of my work and life. My ongoing challenge has been not only how can I live consciously in my day-to-day family life and work, but also how can I translate key principles and techniques from the wisdom tradition into language that makes sense to people's ordinary experience, and can be applied for greater effectiveness and success at work. In this sense, my most creative work is as a translator.

I have found useful concepts and tools consistent with the wisdom tradition in a number of contemporary secular disciplines applicable to the work setting:

- Personal growth, human potential studies, high performance psychology;
- Mindbody studies, holistic health, psychoneuroimmunology;
- Whole systems theory, computers and information technology; ecological sciences, chaos studies, and other "new paradigm" sciences;
- Interpersonal relationships and communication.

Drawing upon these fields, I have developed an approach relevant to the key areas of corporate consulting, coaching, and training I provide:

- Individual high performance and empowerment;
- Personal well-being and stress management;
- Enlightened, empowering leadership;
- High-performing teams, communication and feedback;
- Change management and organizational revitalization.

My recent emphasis has focused on the first three of these areas, which I cover in more detail in this book.

I have presented this work to a wide range of clients: universities; manufacturing, information technology, and engineering organizations; health care agencies and hospitals; small businesses of many types; school districts; community and human service agencies; and for all levels of individuals and teams, including executive leadership, mid-management, professional, administrative, technical and custodial staff, and plant production workers.

My basic commitment has been to balance the organization's demands for successful change and high performance with the individual's needs for well-being, freedom, and fulfillment at work. To tap the creative spirit that brings out the best in people and organizations, I have developed an integrated approach consisting of three key processes:

- Awareness of essential principles
- Cultivation of individual qualities
- Mastery of a personal technology of transformation

People can apply these processes to enhance skillfulness, effectiveness, and satisfaction at work. At advanced stages of mastery, they can be the springboard to self-realization and freedom. While most of my work has focused on introductory and intermediate areas, recently I am beginning to see an authentic desire from more clients to enter more fully into the transformative and transcendental experience for the deepest and most lasting results.

Essential Principles

A number of key underlying principles and beliefs from the wisdom tradition provide the basic context for all my work. I discuss these in varying degrees of specificity, sometimes stating them explicitly, often just implying them, depending on the context and the audience:

Change & Impermanence

If we pay close attention to life, it becomes obvious that everything in the phenomenal universe is changing. Life is an ongoing flow of transformation and impermanence, a continual process of becoming in which everything is being born, growing, maturing, decaying, dying. The seasons come and go, the heavenly bodies revolve and rotate, and our work schedules, positions, processes, technologies, and organizational structures are being continually revised.

Not only is everything changing, but the very rate of change itself is accelerating. We find ourselves now in the midst of a vast social transformation equal in force and speed to the transition from the European Middle Ages to the Renaissance and Reformation. Driven as much as anything by the brilliant innovations in computers and information technology, this acceleration is perhaps best captured in Gordon Moore's famous law that CPU processor speed doubles every eighteen months. The relentless intensification of technological and organizational change in corporate America is showing up in our work lives in the incessant demands to work faster, eat faster, drive faster, speak faster, to get it all done and keep up with the competition.

The current speed and flux is bringing us face to face with the injunctions of the ancient sages that we must recognize and accept the reality of unpredictable change in order to become fully creative participants in the flow. Because change is in our very lifeblood, it is painful to resist the fundamental natural order. To oppose the new, to cling to the old that is disappearing, is a primary source of our suffering. It both expresses and sustains the sense of a radically separate self that seeks fixity and solidity in the midst of fluidity. Acceptance of change allows us to live in harmony with the natural flow, to find our appropriate pace and ultimate identity with the whole.

In the workplace today this full embrace of flux is at the heart of successful change management, continuous improvement, and organizational and individual resilience. This awareness of ongoing impermanence—which was originally associated mostly with Buddhism and Taoism—is supported by the brilliant understandings coming from whole systems theory on how self-organizing systems undergo periods of intense stress as the catalyst toward higher levels of complexity and adaptability. As Margaret Wheatley succinctly puts it: "Life uses messes to get to well-ordered solutions." Systems thinking is the next upgrade in the formulation of perennial wisdom, giving us a lucid theory of the paradoxes of order and chaos and a more advantageous perspective from which to understand how organizations change.

Into this swirling mix I fold the Judaeo-Christian serenity prayer of Reinhold Niebuhr:

> God, grant me the serenity to accept the things I cannot change, the courage to change the things I can, and the wisdom to know the difference.

The wisdom to distinguish between what you can and cannot change or control is basic to effectiveness. Work life today is a daily challenge to cultivate this wisdom: to know when to act decisively in the midst of ambiguity, to know when to abandon ineffective strategies, to know when to persist or when to move on. Our ability to apply this polarity is strengthened by a striking corollary to the serenity prayer, the Taoist balance of yin and yang which describes the two complementary forces that together drive the wheel of life. Seen in terms of individual qualities, the yang—i.e, the courage to change what we can—is the courageous, proactive, responsible, goal-oriented, rational masculine principle; the yin—the serenity to accept what we cannot change—is the flexible, intuitive, flowing, receptive, patient, feminine mode. Balancing these forces within us creates the resilience necessary to stay grounded and responsive in the ongoing flux. It reveals our wholeness and allows us to express our full creative power to capitalize on the opportunity within change.

Unity and Interdependence

The great power of the perennial wisdom is in the radical simplicity of its holistic vision, a brilliant, penetrating awareness that sees through the appearance of multiplicity and separation to the underlying unity and interdependence of existence. Everything and everyone are seen to be interrelated aspects of a vast whole system. As the Roman Stoic philosopher Marcus Aurelius described it:

> Constantly regard the universe as one living being, having one substance and one soul; and observe how all things have reference to one perception, the perception of this one living being; and how all things act with one movement; and how all things are the cooperating causes of all things which exist; observe too the continuous spinning of the thread and the contexture of the web.

Our current fascination and involvement with the Web, Internet, computer connectivity, telecommunication networks, and interpersonal networking are vivid contemporary iterations of this ancient awareness of our interdependent unity. Whether we call it the Body of Christ, the Great Chain of Being, Gaia, deep ecology, or self-organizing systems, we are referring to a vision of synthesis that heals the old dualism—the analytical perception that divides the inherent wholeness of existence into bits and parts. Nowadays we are discovering the many dimensions of our interconnectedness: the holistic unity of the self-regulating individual bodymind organism, immersed in the ecological interdependence of nature, wired into the latticed network of global electronic connectivity. We are awakening to our existence as a vast network in which the apparent parts are seen to be embedded in a wider wholeness.

The science of environmental studies and philosophy of deep ecology are revealing the full interdependence of organism and environment. We see there are no fixed separate entities called "environment" or "organism" but rather a network of relationships that continually interpenetrate, influence, and change one another. Life is a reciprocity and circularity where everything fits in the totality.

The holistic vision sees the human being as an inseparable expression of the whole. Within the totality there are distinctions of form, but no real separation into parts. As Alan Watts liked to point out, we don't come into life, we come out of it just as a leaf comes out of a tree: The so-called *boundary* of the skin literally *joins* us to life within a larger, ecological symbiosis. In the Perennial Philosophy the classic image is that we are all waves of the ocean, each of us a temporary form of the underlying formless reality that is our ultimate Self.

The unity of existence is reflected in the work setting when people recognize that their survival, success, and well-being at work depend on their mutual reliance in a collaborative whole system. I emphasize a vision of wholes-within-wholes, in which each whole includes and transcends the wholes integrated within it: the self-managing, self-motivated aware individual; the successful team as a whole system of interdependent, supportive, responsible individuals committed to one another and to their purpose; the organization as a self-organizing whole system of individuals, teams and departments—strengthened by collectively defining its mission, vision, values, core competencies and operating procedures, and then by living self-referentially, consistent with its collective identity. Finally, we look at how the organization is a fully interdependent part of a wider, global unity consisting of the environment, external customers and the world economy, technological innovation and telecommunications to which it is constantly responding and adapting.

To resist unity or interdependence at any level creates the possibility of ineffectiveness or more serious dysfunction in that system. Personal ignorance of the mutual influence of mind and body can destroy our health. Highly competitive individualism can hinder or destroy team-work, and undermine the trust essential to organizational flow and morale. The dualistic belief in a radically separate individual strug-gling to survive, so deeply embedded in our cultural heritage, is the primary cause of our personal suffering and a constant centripetal force in our relationships and organizational behavior.

One great challenge at work today is to discover the subtle balance between individuality and collective harmony, between self-interest and the good of the whole. As we acknowledge our unity we can experi-ence our own inherent wholeness and also live in harmony with oth-ers. When we speak of accepting diversity, for example, we are not only expressing our appreciation of individual people, styles, and cul-tures. We are recognizing the underlying unity and how it differenti-ates itself into the rich variety of form. Celebrating diversity is literally an act of praise for the magnificence of creation and the creative Source itself.

Interestingly, the reality of underlying unity is not static, but a dy-namic process of wholes-within-wholes evolving toward greater inte-gration, self-knowledge, and effectiveness. As we honor and develop interdependence, we empower each concentric whole system to attain greater internal effectiveness and respond more appropriately to its context. People, teams, and organizations each have a spiritual path that is the unfolding of their inherent potential.

The Human Potential

According to the Perennial Philosophy, the essence of the human be-ing is the universal Self, the absolute being-consciousness-energy which manifests as each individual and all of life. One quality of the Self is energy or power—the vibrant, dynamic potentiality which is the source of all our experience. I usually refer to this deep reservoir of resource-fulness within us as the human potential, the power, ability, creativity, and talent that is available to each of us for accomplishment, happiness, and fulfillment in our lives and work. I view it as pure possibility, a coding within each of us—call it genetics, karma, God's will, or destiny—that represents all we could become, individually and collectively.

Like the oak tree encoded in the acorn, within each human being is a design for full actualization in this life. If the acorn falls on fertile soil and receives the right nutrients, it can indeed become a great tree. Work can be a fertile opportunity to nurture this growth. It is leadership's role to provide the environment, resources, and encouragement to release this potential, as it is the individual's responsibility to acknowledge the inner power and to go for it. It is up to each individual to choose to actualize the possibility and express it in their life and work.

This potential is literally the vital energy that drives our thoughts, feelings, and behaviors. When we take responsibility for this force, we can channel it and ride it to empowerment and peak performance. This is the source of self-motivation, enthusiasm, and morale at work. When we disown it, we live as if we are powerless victims, which shows up as complaining, negativity, helplessness, and dependency in the workplace. The most critical challenge to many of us at work is to make the shift in sense of self from victim to agent, from effect to cause, of our experience and success.

Almost every day in my work we have this dialogue about who we are and what we are capable of. Challenging and often risky, it is the ongoing meditation that can release the power we need to rise to the occasion.

The Power of Awareness

My main work is supporting people and their organizations to be aware. Awareness gives people freedom, power, and choice, strengthening their ability to change. Unconsciousness sustains the repetition of automatic patterns of behavior, both individual and organizational, that impede learning and limit growth and success.

In the wisdom tradition, awareness is an essential property of the Self. To be fully aware is to realize one's nature as consciousness itself. Not only is it the ultimate spiritual act to be conscious, it is also a practical tool for success and skillfulness in the work setting. For the individual, self-reflection and introspection are the bases for self-knowledge and personal and professional development. Listening and paying attention to others provide clear seeing into the nature of people and their behavior, communications, relationships, and work processes. Openness to learning and awareness-raising activities—through education and training, coaching and mentoring, formal and informal feedback processes—is crucial to continuous improvement and the empowerment of the work force. As mentioned in the previous chapter, awareness as information is literally the aliveness and creativity that activates the group potential for adapting rapidly to internal and external challenges.

Mind Creates Experience

"Mind" in the perennial wisdom is a collective term usually referring to the many forms that consciousness takes. The underlying ocean of consciousness gives rise to waves—thoughts, attitudes, opinions, values, beliefs, interpretations, concepts, and so on—that channel our formless potentiality into specific experiences.

Mind as so understood is a two-edged sword that can either limit or expand our potential. Our deepest, mostly unconscious, interpretations—assumptions, beliefs, values, self-images, desires, and fears—have the greatest power to shape and direct the energy of our thoughts, feelings, and behaviors. What we are unaware of controls us. As we become aware enough to see the unconscious conditioned mechanisms of mind that drive experience, we have the power and choice to change our experience and behavior, both individually and collectively. This awareness gives us the freedom to identify obstacles and limitations to resolve or accept, acknowledge our strengths and true values, and consciously choose areas for development. We can envision a future and co-create it.

If this awareness is shared collectively in the workplace, it may also allow people to realize that they have the power, literally, to imagine the organization. The group dialogue on vision, mission, values, and operating principles can create a collective mind that shapes organizational experience and behavior consistent with our true nature and deepest commitments. The huge challenge here is to see that mind can become our instrument rather than our master. If people learn to use their minds wisely, they can develop the qualities and master the techniques for fulfillment and effectiveness at work.

Cultivation of Individual Qualities

Implementing these principles requires a commitment to self-development that strengthens both the individual and the organization. Like the American Transcendentalists Emerson, Thoreau, and Whitman, who celebrated the simple values and noble virtues, my focus is on the relationship between honoring your being and doing good work. I emphasize the cultivation of certain qualities—core competencies or characteristics of successful people—that are the basis of the high-performing, empowered work force that organizations are demanding today. By developing these qualities individuals can release their potential for professional effectiveness and personal growth. Carried to maturity, these characteristics generate and express the fullness of what we call self-actualization.

These characteristics can be divided into a) personal qualities that support individual empowerment, and b) interpersonal competencies conducive to collaborative interdependence and teamwork within the collective organization. Developed together, they provide the foundations for a "spirituality of democracy" which balances enlightened individualism and harmonious community for the greatest good of all. This balance, which we have been seeking in American society for the past two hundred years, is now appropriate for the success and well-being of our businesses and organizations.

In my courses and coaching I engage people in applying these qualities to their specific work context. I seek a balance that supports people to understand the relevance of these characteristics to the work, to identify personal and organizational obstacles to their implementation, and to learn specific skill-building exercises that develop the quality. Chapter four describes how I see some of the individual qualities operating in inspired leaders.

INDIVIDUAL	INTERPERSONAL
Self-awareness	Interdependence
Values	Communication
Integrity	Acceptance
Responsibility	Compassion
Self-Acceptance	Trust
Courage	Appreciation
Resilience	Support
Commitment	Collaboration
Detachment	Leadership
Play	The Empowering Stand

Mastery of the Technology of Transformation

These qualities remain nice-sounding abstractions until we put them into practice through the application of specific tools. In the great spiritual traditions or peak performance disciplines, it is the committed, regular practice of exercises and techniques that builds the desired skills or outcomes. Without meditation there is no Zen, for example, and what is Christianity without praise and prayer? Stress management is likewise empty talk without relaxation techniques, and listening skills are required for good communication. Drawing upon the wide range of experience in the perennial tradition, I have provided a set of tools that people can practice at work to develop the desired skills and channel their creative energy for both individual and organizational success. Here is an overview of these techniques. Details for many of them are in chapter six.

Stress management tools: the isness of business

The continuing need for stress management in the workplace provides the easiest opportunity for introducing practices that for millennia people have used to let go and be energized. If we can't get away from work to retreat to the mountain top, then we bring the mountain to work. "Stress" is our society's somewhat denatured term for what the Buddha called *dukkha,* the fundamental suffering of life inherent in clinging to our desires, fears, and survival mentality.

I am continually impressed with how powerful these simple tools are for relieving our suffering and giving direct access to peace and well-being. Stress management has come to include ways to center and relax, access inner knowing and intuition, release and transform stress and emotional upsets, reorganize our lives, and promote our health. It enables us to find the unchanging center—the eye of the storm—in the midst of the swirling, accelerating pace of life. This ground of quiet being gives us true rest and revitalizes us for our productive work.

Specific practices I have taught regularly through the years include:

• Breath awareness meditation for centering and relaxation
• Self-awareness, or mindfulness, of thoughts, feelings, behaviors
• Body scan for dealing with emotions and sensations
• Music meditation
• Silence
• Yoga postures

Mind tools for creating the possible

A number of dynamic mental techniques enable people to develop qualities and skills that enhance their personal development and professional performance. Drawn originally from the spiritual paths and secularized through the language of personal growth, high performance athletic training, and holistic health therapies, they are extraordinarily potent tools for proactively creating experience in many areas of our lives. In these sessions, often high energy experiences for the participants, we integrate left-brain reshaping of positive thought processes, and right-brain holistic imaging:

• Positive self-talk, empowering beliefs and affirmations
• Visualization and guided imagery, team and organizational
   visioning.

Although on the surface, communication may seem purely utilitarian, I have found teaching the simple elements of effective communication to be a profoundly spiritual process. The word "communication" itself derives from the same root as "commune," "communion," and "community." It literally refers to what we share in common. Communication thus describes the flow of consciousness within the undivided totality, the way the One speaks to itself, shares itself, knows itself. When people practice basic communication tools, they not only build the skills for working together interdependently, they can also come to know one another in ways that can reveal their shared unity. The key communication techniques I emphasize are:

- Listening
- Integrity, self-expression and assertiveness
- Constructive feedback, recognition and praise
- Conflict management skills

Not only do these constitute effective work-group communication, they circulate the love and intelligence of the conscious organization. Listening is the basis for meditation that opens one to greater knowing, while integrity and assertive self-expression release transformative energies. Feedback and managing conflict skills are instruments of compassion, service, and peacemaking on the job.

The Balance of Being and Doing

The ultimate point of my work is to create a balance of skillful doing and conscious being. I often approach this with a discussion of how to marry two apparently opposite qualities: being engaged and being detached.

How can we be energetically, proactively committed at work while at the same time see it all from a transcendental perspective that doesn't cling to changing appearances? How can we give work our best shot and engage in continuous improvement, yet not be painfully attached to the stressful perfectionism that dogs our efforts toward high performance? That is, can we find our identity and well-being in the underlying perfection that can never be measured or quantified? Can we take our work seriously and yet joyfully express the light spirit of play and humor? How can we want the very best for ourselves, our co-workers and our organizations and still accept the fleeting ups and downs of this changing manifestation?

As we find our interior answers to these questions and grok the mystery of how to be in the world but not of it, we approach the integration Robert Frost describes so movingly:

> But yield who will to their separation,
> My object in living
> Is to unite my avocation and my vocation,
> As my two eyes make one in sight.
> Only where love and need are one,
> And the work is play for mortal stakes,
> Is the deed ever really done
> For heaven and the future's sakes.

> —Robert Frost
> "Two Tramps in Mudtime"

Frost boldly calls us to face our experience of work in the brilliant light of his uncompromising, unitive stand. Here is the holistic vision that sees through the illusory separation to the underlying unity, that sees there can be an integration of our calling and what we enjoy doing. This integration arises directly from our willingness to be open and allow the unfolding of the destiny encoded within us. This is both a receptivity to experience fully what seeks to manifest through us, as well as it is a committed, conscious choice we make, an accepting embrace of work and ourself. We see our work here as self-expression, as the activity of our creativity and a vehicle of our desire to contribute.

The new, radical bottom line Frost announces so emphatically—only where love and need are one!—joins the need to make a living and our enthusiasm for what we do. It joins our need to express our talents and drive for success with our caring for and valuing the people we work with. The balance of mind and heart, intellect and emotion, survival and contribution releases the greatest wisdom and power for effective performance and harmony with others.

Perhaps even more challenging to our deepest, most unconscious survival strategies is the poet's full-bodied invocation of play for mortal stakes. Work is clearly serious business, with money, security, sometimes life and death at stake in the decisions and actions that we take daily. And yet, how can it be play? I was especially amazed, during the five years I worked closely with hospitals and the nursing profession, that even in the midst of the most intense, high risk dramas, these committed medical professionals could—indeed, had to for their own sanity—see the humor and take it lightly. Similarly, in the world of investment and the wheeling and dealing of corporate mergers, some of the great entrepreneurs also play the game of work and business, and the higher the stakes and the risks, the more they enjoy it.

We can free up and sustain the light spirit of adventure and fun when we keep a wider perspective. "The world is a playground for the wise and a graveyard for the foolish," said Poonjaji. Or, from an equally profound teacher on how to live free and joyful in the midst of our daily chores, Mary Poppins sings: "In every job that must be done, there is an element of fun. You find the fun and snap! the job's a game."

The wisdom tradition reminds us that life is indeed a play. In heeding Shakespeare's reminder that "all the world's a stage, and all the men and women merely players," can you play your role effectively and yet remember you are the Being behind all the roles, witnessing your own play?

The answer to that question, I believe, is what Frost was referring to by "is the deed every really done for heaven and the future's sakes." Only when these conditions are in place will the deed ever really be done in harmony with our deepest calling and spiritual vision. As we see our work reflecting our true values and expressing our integrity we can become aware of its transcendental meaning and role in the larger flow and playing out of destiny. When we view our work as spiritual activity and communion, we can wake up to its ultimate nature as the play of consciousness itself.

Waking Up

The Perennial Philosophy emphasizes that the purpose of life is to wake up: to realize who we are, and to experience the fullness possible in the human condition. Its teachers describe an ultimate state of human development, which has been given many names—enlightenment, self-realization, cosmic consciousness, unitive awareness. The danger of such esoteric language is to make this sound somehow unattainable to most people, a distant otherworldly mystery only accessible to rare mystics, rather than your most intimate and immediate presence, your very birthright as a human being. Edward Carpenter expresses it eloquently:

> If you inhibit thought (and persevere) you come at length to a region of consciousness below or behind thought . . . and a realization of an altogether vaster self than that to which we are accustomed. And since the ordinary consciousness, with which we are concerned in daily life, is before all things founded on the little local self . . . to pass out of that is to die to the ordinary self and the ordinary world. It is to die in the ordinary sense, but in another, it is to wake up and find the "I," one's real, most intimate self, pervades the Universe and all other things—that the mountains and the sea and the stars are a part of one's body and that one's soul is in touch with the souls of all creatures.

The awakening shows up as the experience of being home, the deep relief and familiar sense of being who you really are. It is grounded in a stable inner peace, equanimity, and the joy of knowing that this happiness is your nature. There is the intuitive knowing of the mystery of life itself. You exist as a spacious, timeless presence in the here and now. The experience of wholeness flows out expansively as a pervading sense of relatedness with everyone in the wider totality that is our ultimate identity.

This non-dual, or unitive, realization is the heart of the perennial wisdom: the recognition that there is not-two, that there is no separation in the seamless web of all manifestation. It is the undeniable knowing that a supreme underlying reality manifests as the physical universe. The spiritual and the material, in no way separate, are both expressions of the same essence. The issue is not to bring spirit into life, rather it is to live in the wisdom that all life is already a manifestation of the invisible source.

The essence of individual realization is precisely that there is no individual "I" separate from this totality. It is a clear knowing that who we are is not restricted to the mindbody organism with which we have identified throughout our life. It sees clearly that ego—the attachment to the "I" thought and identification with the survival functions of the bodymind organism—creates the experience of being separate from the Self and is the root cause of human suffering. Self-realization does not deny individuality, only separation. It is an awakening from the egoic drama of separate individuality to the reality that each of us is a wave on the ocean of the universal Self, an expression of that which is manifesting as everyone.

The awakening is both a fulfillment of individuality and a self-transcendence. You realize that you are the individual and the whole simultaneously, freed up to be here and live fully. Awakening is not the end of the game, rather it is the beginning of forever, a forever in which the inherent potential within us unfolds as destiny.

From this unhurried realization we see that work is our play and joy, the way we participate in the ongoing creation of the universe and make our lasting contribution to life. Today's democratization of consciousness makes the workplace a legitimate—and necessary—domain of this awakening, and an opportunity to share this experience with others.

In the knowing of this unity our experience of others is love. The compassionate acceptance of all life and living beings is the natural way we relate when we realize that everyone and everything is our Self. When merged in the totality, individual self-interest intuitively becomes one with the interest of all, and the actions of the awakened one spontaneously serve the well-being of the whole. Enlightened action is by its very nature appropriately responsive to the circumstance.

This transformation is the paradoxical process of becoming what you always-already are. It is not a matter of attaining something new, but of recognizing what is. It is a direct seeing into one's own nature.

Not an evolutionary way, it sees through all levels, dimensions, phases, stages to what is already complete here and now. You cannot attain what you already are, you can only realize it. This is the power of the wisdom path, the path of insight or knowledge. It is the pathless path. Since there is no way to arrive at where you already are, all you can do is be.

The heart of the non-dual realization is the recognition that there is a single reality which is the source, substratum, and true nature of everything. Ultimate mystery without quality or measure, beginning or end, prior to time and space itself, nothing can be said about it. Yet still we speak: in its formless essence it is all-pervading being-consciousness-energy; in form it manifests as the universe and all beings, all life. This underlying reality, both transcendent and immanent, is the true nature of everyone and everything, visible and invisible, manifest and unmanifest.

What is called enlightenment is the direct experience that you are this Mystery, awake to its eternal presence. "I am That I am" is its own intuition of itself, a conscious space in which joy, peace, and love exist as the unbroken context within which the temporary waves of bodymind experience arise and dissolve. This being-consciousness sees itself in everything, knows that all manifestations, all worlds, all beings arise as expressions of its own self-nature.

IV

AWAKENING LEADERSHIP

Soul, individual spirituality, firsthand personal insight into things, the courage to be oneself and go the way one's conscience points, humility in the face of the mysterious order of Being, confidence in its natural direction and, above all, trust in one's own subjectivity as the principal link with the subjectivity of the world—these, in my view, are the qualities that [leaders] of the future should cultivate.

—*Vaclav Havel*

The Spirit of Leadership

Leadership has a crucial role in the awakening of consciousness in the workplace. First, leaders must take a stand that it is desirable and create the opportunity and conditions for it. Secondly, and most importantly, they must model the way. There is no substitute for leading by example. As Mahatma Gandhi said, "Each of us must be the change we want to see in the world." Albert Schweitzer was uncompromising on this fundamental demand on leadership: "Example is not the main thing in influencing others; it is the only thing."

In appreciating the demands placed on leaders today, I've come to see leadership as a spiritual activity as rigorous and transforming as the way of the monk, the sage, the servant, the priestess. Like these traditional archetypes, the leadership role in the workplace is an opportunity to realize and express the fullness of our original nature. If our commitment is to be awake in our daily lives and work, then we can engage leadership as a transformational process for becoming conscious and actualizing our full potential, as well as for sharing that awakening and leading others to realization as well.

We are also beginning to look at leadership, not in the traditional sense as an individual or a position, but as Margaret Wheatley reminds us in her vision of emergent organizations, "Leaders emerge and recede as needed. Leadership is a series of behaviors rather than a role for heroes." Leadership, then, is a set of principles and techniques that anyone, regardless of position, can perform—and, indeed, may need to—as the flattening of organizations and increased use of high performance work systems empowers more employees with leadership functions.

There has been a growing emphasis recently in the voluminous organizational literature on the spiritual nature of leadership. I was first moved by the reference to leadership as a spiritual activity in the distinction Warren Bennis and Burt Nanus make between management and leadership. While the distinctions may be overgeneralized, they do highlight essential differences in the two activities.

In essence, they point out, managers do things right while leaders do the right thing. There is an intangible moral, ethical connotation to leadership. Deriving from the Latin words *mano* and *manus* for "hand," management focuses on handling, supervising, or being in charge of. Leadership, from the Anglo-Saxon *lithan* meaning "to go," is about guiding or influencing in direction. Management primarily maintains what is—systems, procedures and routine—while leadership proactively creates the new. To lead is to envision the future, look ahead, foresee, invent, design, plan, imagine what is next. This visionary capacity—the prophetic quality in the Judaeo-Christian tradition—is indispensable to leadership. There is no activity more spiritual than envisioning and participating in the process of creation, giving shape to the unfolding future. Rather than living reactively, at the effect of forces out of their control, leaders live as cause. Be they politicians, business leaders, athletic coaches, or musical conductors, their commitment is to work with the resources available to bring out the new. Whether they invent it, channel it, co-create it, or articulate the inchoate desires of the people, leaders abide in the causal domain.

As Joe Jaworski summarizes it well: "The conventional view of leadership emphasizes positional power and conspicuous accomplishment. But true leadership is about creating a domain in which we continually learn and become more capable of participating in our unfolding future. A true leader thus sets the stage on which predictable miracles, synchronistic in nature, can—and do—occur."

Bennis and Nanus point out that whereas managers focus on the how to—on the practical and details—leaders emphasize the why: the values, meaning, and purpose of the big picture. Leadership is about identity and meaning: who we are, what we stand for, why we are doing this. While managers are responsible for mobilizing the physical resources to get things done, leaders go deeper to mobilize emotional and spiritual resources. They do this by tapping and reflecting peoples' aspirations, commitment, trust, and esteem for themselves and one another. They inspire, empower, and nurture people. As Bennis and Nanus indicate, managers may get people to do things, but leaders get people to want to do things. Leadership is in touch with the deeper underpinnings of motivation. Finally, managers implement the plan, while leaders model the way. Integrity is the *sine qua non* of leadership, and increasingly in our society today, the litmus test for survival in office.

I was equally moved by Peter Block's emphasis on stewardship and Richard Greenleaf's concept of servant leadership. These complementary views envision leadership as guided by a set of principles and values focused on serving a larger community and the well-being of others. As Block described it, "The revolution is also about the belief that spiritual values and the desire for economic success can be simultaneously fulfilled. Stewardship taken seriously is not just an economic strategy or a way to achieve higher levels of productivity or to succeed in a marketplace. It is also an answer to the spirit calling out."

Stewardship refers to holding something in trust for another—in this case, holding and developing the resources of the organization for the well-being of all. Service and stewardship imply a fundamental shift from pursuing self-interest to focusing on the benefit of others and the good of the whole. It involves a sharing of power and leadership functions with others, while at the same time the leader remains ultimately accountable for the success of the larger organization. Acting out of service, not control, calls for a new way of operating that trusts people's inherent talents and potential, and supports everyone to work on themselves. It calls for the practice of humility which has traditionally been one of the absolute preconditions for spiritual life and which undermines the egotism or arrogance usually associated with traditional macho models of leadership. Ultimately, leadership as a spiritual path is not about you at all, but about transcending the sense of separateness by giving yourself to something larger and deeper. In that giving of oneself, the true Self deeper than ego is revealed.

The emphasis on service and stewardship is functionally equivalent to the bodhisattva vow in Buddhism. The bodhisattva, or advanced practitioner, makes a commitment to work for the well-being of all beings, and literally postpones his or her own final enlightenment until everyone is saved. While on the surface this may seem like the "right" thing to do, in truth Buddhism very subtly recognizes that caring about people frees practitioners from their egoic concerns, thus fostering one's own realization in the process of serving others.

Karmacology

The path of service—be it the Buddhist approach, the Hindu emphasis on karma yoga, or the Judaeo-Christian attitude toward charity and good works—has a deep foundation in the flow of circularity within the interdependence of life. It follows the law of cause and effect in a whole system, which I am calling karmacology (karma + ecology), a fusion of eastern and western understandings of the operation of unity. It recognizes that within life there is a circulating flow of energy, power, or love. In a whole system, as we say, what goes around, comes around. What you put out there comes back to you. It is the Biblical wisdom: You reap what you sow. If you put out love, truth, power, nourishment, ultimately, somehow, they come back to you.

Karmacology reveals a unitive vision that sees through the scarcity mentality of egoic self-interest to the abundance of the totality. Our view of reality—what we think is "out there"—is a function of the individual mind. We see the world in our own image. If we identify as the incomplete, egoic self, we will see a world of scarcity in which we must struggle to get what we need. If we live knowing we are the totality itself, we see abundance and experience fulfillment, and thus a willingness to share what we have. The poverty model of thinking, based on the neediness of the egoic self, continually senses that there is not enough to go around. The mentality of abundance knows that there is plenty and gives accordingly. When we realize the wholeness within us, then we will experience the abundance available to everyone around us and share it willingly. Abundance is a reflection of our inner experience of wholeness, fulfillment, satisfaction.

Scarcity thinking sees people as separate, limited containers who can hold just so much within them. In this thinking to give is to deplete, so relationships with others are viewed as exchanges designed to get back what we have given, to replenish our supply that was depleted in the giving. The poverty mind is thus attached to returns; relationship becomes a manipulation to get what you need, and generates resentment or blame when those we have given to do not return our gifts. Since subliminally the scarcity mentality is predisposed to believe that there is never enough, this produces a constant tension. Even when we get what we want from others, we are still attached and insecure, fearing loss.

In the mindset of abundance, people, rather than viewed as separate, are known to be joined in a larger unity. Rather than viewing ourselves as limited containers, we can see ourselves as vessels through which the flow can circulate unobstructed. If we are open to the flow, we see that to give is to receive, and that the more we give it away, the more we have it. This realization is the basis for true unconditional giving—which seeks not for exchange or reciprocity from those we give to, but is fulfilled in the act of giving. This, of course, also requires a willingness to receive. Otherwise, we get caught in the co-dependent trap of having to be the giver, the helper, but not open to receiving. Rather than the tension, frustration, or resentment of the scarcity mentality, in the abundance mode we live in gratitude for what we are receiving, gratitude for the miraculous existence of this fulfillment and the grace of having discovered it within us. This is the deepest basis for the generosity of the leader as steward and servant.

Empowerment: Sharing the Gift of Power

The circular process of giving and sharing is critical to the path of leadership. Lee Bolman and Terry Deal have shown that leaders share certain spiritual gifts with people. I would like to emphasize that the fundamental gifts leaders have to share are qualities of their own true nature—among them power, love, and truth. The very sharing of them reinforces their existence within us.

Power, traditionally, has been the characteristic most identified with leadership. The power of position, wealth, status, authority; the power to make decisions, to hire and fire, buy and sell; the power to affect the careers, livelihoods, and well-being of people in the organization; the power to build and destroy companies, empires, economic systems, global fortunes. Frankly, my interest in working with leadership is precisely that they have access to such power, and thus, have the greatest ability to make a difference in the lives of many people by using their power wisely and compassionately for the greatest good of all.

We have already pointed out that power or potentiality is an inherent characteristic of the Self. I am speaking literally of the energy underlying the universe: the same awesome force that is locked up in the atom is also within each human being. This power is neutral, and can be channeled either toward destructive or constructive purposes. Our crucial learning for the twenty-first century is how to handle this power appropriately. In the same way, after centuries of traditional command and control hierarchical approaches, we are just now beginning to explore how to share organizational power wisely.

The issue for leadership is to discover how to use your power wisely and compassionately to make a difference with others, how to empower and bring out the best in others in a way that meets both organizational needs for high performance and individual needs for well-being and freedom in work. Ultimately, how to use your power to awaken others to their fullest potential and true self.

Everyone has power within them, whether we refer to it as strength, force, energy, capacity, potential, ability to produce results. Besides the inherent power within, power is also catalyzed socially and culturally through learning and the acquisition of knowledge, the development of skills, and control of information and resources. Power can be used for control, coercion, repression and oppression, or it can be used to influence, develop, educate, liberate. Peter Block pointed out that the power of the boss is asymmetrical: It is easier to tighten up and shrink down an organization and make people cautious, than it is to use power to open up, expand, and make people more courageous. When you try to open up an organization you get to see how power is really dispersed throughout.

It is crucial for the leader to understand the old adage, "power corrupts," as an essentially spiritual insight into how power affects consciousness. Power corrupts when it is used for strictly selfish purposes. Egoic power becomes a limitation to awakening, an obstacle to experiencing the love, humility, and openness of one's essential nature. When leaders understand ego and its survival strategies, they will understand how it serves them and others to share power appropriately for the good of all, rather than hoarding and accumulating it. Sharing power effectively not only supports people to realize their own power within; it also frees the individual leader to be continually energized by the inner source. This is the mutual benefit of authentic empowerment.

Given the shift from hierarchical to flatter, more matrixed organizations today, the big question for leadership is "How to lead in a networked world?" In the wake of downsizing and ongoing reorganization, we are witnessing the emergence of empowerment and high-performance work systems, self-directed teams, and the like in which employees are being asked to take on more management functions and behaviors. More people have the opportunity to act as leaders.

A new form of distributed leadership is evolving which—as Don Tapscott has pointed out—is functionally equivalent to the move from the mainframe to distributed desktop computing, a process which is providing the access to information that is contributing to the shift in leadership. Knowledge is power, and power—as in the control of information—is flowing through the computer networks, LANs, and intranets. Leadership is being redefined as a collective function in which more individuals with greater access to information, regardless of hierarchical level, are given decision-making authority.

As Wheatley observes, "If you think of life as a network, then you don't have bottoms or tops. Emergent solutions can come from anywhere, but they are always very situational, always highly contextual, and therefore they're going to be quite variable, and always unplanned." This is both the great adventure and the great risk of empowerment. If leadership functions are distributed in the organization, we must be ready for the surprises of truly creative solutions.

This new ripple in the flow of power mirrors the shift in consciousness brought about by the expanded presence of women and feminine qualities in organizations. We could describe this as a shift from the traditional, hierarchical, patriarchal power of the charismatic individual to the more networked approach reflecting feminine ways of exercising power. The feminine, or yin, while just as powerful, operates differently than the male. While there are clear limits to generalizations about gender differences, it is not totally amiss to say that feminine modalities—grounded in more subtle interpersonal skills and more willing to engage in collective sharing, dialogue, consensus, and win-win approaches, rather than overt control, command, and the zero-sum game—are definitely affecting the traditional exercise of power, and having their impact on the spread of empowerment. The infusion of feminine approaches allows power to flow more equitably and reach more people in the organization.

Empowerment is the way that leaders invite employees to play the game of co-creation. It occurs successfully through a conscious process of distributing authority and encouraging accountability to release the full power of each individual. Authority and accountability are the two poles between which the current of empowerment flows. This can only work if it is supported by a clear dialogue and agreement among the members of the organization. I have seen well-intentioned empowerment initiatives fail in the absence of clear communication in which expectations, requests, and promises were misunderstood or changed arbitrarily.

If empowerment is to succeed, both the organization and the individual must make and keep their commitments with one another. It is up to leadership to provide opportunity, resources, coaching and mentoring, training and education to support employees to exercise their authority effectively; to trust them, have confidence in their ability, and encourage and support their risk-taking; to create a culture that generates and rewards high performance and empowered action on the part of employees, and recruits and seeks to retain the most self-motivated, creative individuals. On the other hand, it is up to the individuals to commit to the organizational strategy and make a personal choice to be empowered. Their freedom and autonomy reside in their commitment to take full responsibility for being self-motivated, entrepreneurial, and accountable. Empowered employees are willing to sustain their own morale and positive attitude on the job, and take full responsibility for their inner development and career path.

The more all members and stakeholders participate in a meaningful dialogue on the purpose, values, and culture underlying empowerment, the greater will be the performance of all its members. Ultimately high performance is based on the trust built from everyone's willingness for open, honest communication, dialogue, and feedback; for living in integrity and making and keeping clear agreements; for their courage and support for intelligent risk-taking; for mutual respect, valuing individuals and their diversity; and for appreciating, recognizing, and rewarding one another's contributions.

Qualities of the Awakened Leader

Once leaders have created the opportunity for awakening, it is up to them to model the way. This calls for wholeheartedly cultivating the qualities that both realize and express their full potential. Here I'll expand on some of the qualities listed in chapter three that I believe are most aligned with the spiritual nature of leadership.

Self-awareness

The first prerequisite of the awakened leader is self-awareness. The ancient injunction of the Delphic oracle to know thyself before all things is just as relevant today. As Joe Jaworski commented in his wise book on his own awakening as a leader: "Before you can lead others, before you can help others, you have to discover yourself. . . . And nothing is more powerful than someone who knows who they are." Self-knowledge is without doubt the key attribute of leadership. It opens the eye of the storm, the clarity needed in the midst of unpredictable change and increasing ambiguity.

Leadership is the opportunity to come face to face with the two ancient questions underlying the quest for perennial wisdom: Who am I? and What am I doing here? In pursuing this inquiry we not only see how we operate, not only understand what drives us and where we think we are going. We also realize that the deepest knowing of ourselves is indeed the wisdom that we call truth or reality. Self-awareness is a fundamental quality of our true nature and the most direct avenue to realizing it. "We must closely examine the nature of the knower," advises Jean Klein, the Swiss master of non-dual consciousness. "This requires all our attention, all our love. Thus you will discover what you really are. . . . To integrate awareness of the Self is freedom."

If I asked you now the question "Who are you?" how would you answer? Usually we refer to our roles, credentials, occupation, history, gender, bodies, and physical condition. We might invoke our values, ideas, beliefs, perhaps desires and fears. We define our strengths and weaknesses, take tests to determine our "type" and "style." We refer to our nationality, religion, race, class, social status to describe ourselves. We think of the psychological self, the social self, the cultural self, the natural, biological self. A little reflection shows that all these categories and elements that we usually identify with change at different stages of life, all are conditional on circumstances or nature, accidents of fate, or products of conditioning.

What is the Self that doesn't change? What is that which you are that abides while everything else comes and goes, that remains unconditioned? When we explore the fundamental mystery of Self, we can identify three inseparable components of this unchanging, underlying reality of our nature. Like water, which is liquid, transparent, and tasteless, so does the Self have the qualities of being, awareness, and potentiality.

The simple truth of your existence is that you are. Everyone has the experience "I am." You say it and think it constantly: I am happy, I am sad, I am young, I am getting older, I am organized, I am busy, I am successful, I am late for deadlines, I am a leader, etc. This "I am" is the unbroken thread of continuity of your existence. It is the uninterrupted presence that you have always been, while all mindbody experience and circumstances have changed incessantly. At the core you are pure being. It is always here, and wherever you are it is here. This unchanging being, unruffled by experience, is pure peace, satisfaction, fulfillment. It needs nothing and everything is contained within it. All the experience we seek in life is already within us. Our own being is the ground out of which everything comes, the source of all our experience, doing and having.

The Self not only is, it is aware that it is. Consciousness, a fundamental quality of our true nature, is the capacity of sentience—to know, to feel, to think, to intuit, to be aware of our experience. The perennial wisdom declares that consciousness is the underlying substrate of reality and inheres in all life, from the human being to the smallest insects and even inorganic matter. As humans we have an extraordinary capacity to become fully self-aware.

Usually, we think we are the mindbody package and identify with our thoughts, feelings, and bodies. Yet there is something that is aware of all of this, and can witness it without identifying with it or being limited by it. This capacity to witness or observe is pure awareness. Attention is a focusing of awareness on a specific object of experience. Full attention to our experience in the here and now—including thoughts, feelings, behaviors, sensations, environment—is often called mindfulness. It is, in other words, simply listening: listening to yourself, to your experience, to others, and to your surroundings.

This awareness has enormous power. To be aware in this way changes everything. It puts you in full touch with yourself and with life. It brings a penetrating clarity, a way to see things as they really are, without conditioning, prior images, or preconceptions.

Times of change and ambiguity demand that leaders pay full attention to what is emerging in this moment. If you know how to listen, you can discover what to do next. It is such a relief to realize that it's all right not to know what to do next, as long as you are willing to *listen*, open and alert in the moment. This quality of mindfulness in the here and now frees up intuition and is the key to all appropriate response. In full attention, what you need to know will show up and the direction of the flow is revealed.

In his exploration of synchronicity in leadership, Jaworski observed: "The capacity to discover and participate in our unfolding future has more to do with our being—our total orientation of character and consciousness—than what we do. Leadership is about creating, day by day, a domain in which we and those around us continually deepen our understanding of reality and are able to participate in shaping the future. This, then, is the deeper territory of leadership—collectively 'listening' to what is wanting to emerge in the world, and then having the courage to do what is required."

When we focus awareness on our own potentiality, empowerment happens naturally. As discussed in chapter three, this deep reservoir of energy or power within us is another fundamental component of the true Self. It is the formless, dynamic vitality or life force itself, the stuff from which all experience flows. Within this domain of sheer possibility, your destiny is encoded. The challenge to the visionary, self-aware leader is to intuit and embrace that destiny. This embrace is both a proactive choice and a surrender that frees you to live out your potential without resistance.

I am continually struck by how we resist our own potential and hold on to our sense of limitation. This resistance—which on the surface seems like a denial of our power and possibility—is actually founded on a deeper, subliminal awareness of the awesome capacity within us. "Our deepest fear is not that we are inadequate," Marianne Williamson ironically suggests. "Our deepest fear is that we are powerful beyond measure. It is our Light, not our darkness, that most frightens us. . . . And as we let our own Light shine, we unconsciously give other people permission to do the same. As we are liberated from our own fear, our presence automatically liberates others." This realization of what we are capable of is the source of a leader's self-confidence, courage, and charisma, and of his or her ability to empower and inspire others to their own high performance and greatness.

The Self, then—comprised of being, consciousness, and energy—is the source from which all our experience flows. This mindbody that we usually call "myself" actually arises from our self-nature, formed by the dance of energy and consciousness. Our formless potentiality takes the shape that consciousness gives it. When energy flows through the mind-states of consciousness, it becomes the many forms of our experience. In essence, what you put your attention to, you create. As the Buddha reminded us, "We are what we think. All that we are arises with our thoughts. With our thoughts we make the world." In the Biblical tradition, it is expressed in Proverbs 23:7 as: "For as he thinketh in his heart, so is he."

We can develop the qualities essential to successful leadership as we become aware of how consciousness creates our experience. This calls for an understanding of the human operating system that runs the mindbody organism. The revolutionary fields of holistic health and psychoneuroimmunology have been demonstrating how the old dualistic thinking that separates "mind," "body," "emotions," and "spirit" into discrete categories cannot grasp the fundamental complexity of the mindbody unity. These categories are modifications of energy-consciousness which forms the underlying substratum of an intelligent, self-regulating unitary organism that is in constant communication with itself. Thought stimulates neuronal activity in the brain which generates neurochemicals, protein-based chains of amino acids, that flow as neurotransmitters carrying chemical messages to the cells of the body. Cells have receptors which receive and decode the message injected by the neurotransmitter. The cellular reaction then becomes the basis for our physical and emotional experience.

This whole microcosm of experience is the activity of consciousness. While the physical brain is in the head, intelligence—carried by the neurochemical substrate—literally flows throughout the body. Consciousness courses through, and is resident in, every cell of the body and is in continual communication with itself through its self-regulating network. In true holism, mind, emotions, and body are theoretically equal forces which can influence one another. The physical affects consciousness, and vice versa. Therefore, theoretically, we can intervene at any point and affect the rest of the system. Thus food affects mind-states, massage can open up emotions, and psychological therapy can improve the killer-cell count of the immune system and reduce cancer.

Self-awareness in this context means directly observing the power of mind to shape our experience. We must pay close attention to the crucial formative mind-states—assumptions, beliefs, values, operating principles—that shape our sense of identity and determine what is possible for us.

It is also essential that we come to see how mind filters our perception. "We see things not as they are but as we are," Anais Nin reminds us. The condition of the world we see "out there" is a reflection of how we are within. If we have inner conflicts, we see and experience a world of conflict. Thus, we must find peace and joy within ourselves in order to find it in the world, just as we must be able to resolve inner conflict in order to resolve outer conflict. When asked what he was doing to support the peace movement in the 1960s, a great Zen master replied, echoing a traditional Zen insight: "I drink a cup of tea and stop the war."

Not only does the mind filter our perception, it then uses the data we perceive to justify its beliefs and interpretations. When we really recognize how much we like to be right, we see the inherent hardwiring that locks us into patterns of thinking that sustain our limitations and become self-fulfilling justifications. We take great glee in saying "I told you so." We love to be right, even about interpretations that are killing us. Argue for your limitations and they are yours. This is what I discovered working in the field of personal empowerment for over a decade. There are people who would rather be right about how inadequate they are, than leave a comfort zone and self-image that may be painful but is familiar and secure. This is why the willingness to be wrong is a courageous stand and the basis for change and learning.

If we seek to be aware of the obstacles to our full awakening as leaders, we must closely observe the survival functions of mind and the core assumptions that drive them. Basically, mind is an instrument of survival of the bodymind organism. Here we discover the key software that runs the operating system.

Ken Wilber pointed out that as the fundamental unity of life differentiates itself into organisms or "selves," each organism is moved by two apparently opposing drives simultaneously. One thrust is to pursue its survival and success as a separate entity through the quest for *self-actualization*, the development of the full potential of that organism. At the same time the organism is driven by the equal and opposite drive toward *self-transcendence*: It yearns to go beyond its separate existence and regain its sense of unity with the whole, its communion with the ultimate Self. Taken together, self-actualization and self-transcendence form the full process of self-realization.

The two thrusts are driven by a set of interrelated survival assumptions—the beliefs in separation and incompletion. Ironically, these limiting operating principles sustain suffering while they also impel us to go beyond it. The core belief of the dualistic mind-state is that I am a radically separate identity in the world. This assumption itself is the fall from grace, our own apparent departure from the divine state. It is systematically sustained by cultural conditioning, especially in American culture, which is infused with the most extreme version of individualism on the planet. The yearning for self-transcendence and overcoming the separateness of radical individualism is a subliminal force behind all our stress and suffering.

To believe in our separateness means we have forgotten our original fullness. This is actually an accurate subliminal intuition. Ignorant of our true nature, we suspect that we are not whole, not complete, that something is missing. This is what the Biblical tradition calls Original Sin—the sense that we are "off the mark," that something is missing, that this is not it. We then live driven by this nagging, unconscious suspicion which shows up in the belief that I am not complete, not whole and must fulfill myself. Life then becomes a process of seeking what will complete us, what will perfect us. Maslow's hierarchy of needs describes our pursuit of self-actualization through the fulfillment of a sequence of needs.

Once these beliefs are in place, the key survival strategies of desire and fear attempt to overcome separation and incompletion, to regain wholeness and unity. Desire can range along a spectrum of interest-attraction-like-preference-attachment-need-dependency-addiction. We seek whatever we judge will give us the experience of wholeness and communion. As long as we seek these outside ourselves in material objects—fame, fortune, relationship, status, success—we will never be satisfied. The whole economic system and advertising industry promotes a consumerism designed to generate and sustain this fundamental dissatisfaction by dangling in front of us the never-ending promises of more, better and different.

We won't be satisfied until we understand the bottom line about desire: that desire itself is never satisfied. We might experience a temporary gratification when we momentarily obtain a desired object or experience, but the *process* of desire goes on. When we see the mechanism of desire as an endless loop, we can finally see through the whole pattern. While we think it is the gratification of the desire that creates satisfaction, we come to understand that actually it is the absence of desire—the state of desirelessness—that reveals the inherent satisfaction of our true Self.

Your freedom from the endless cycle of desire and gratification comes in the realization that happiness, fulfillment, and satisfaction are already within you. This awareness itself is liberating. Then you can witness the process of desire and gently turn your needs, demands, and attachments into preferences lightly held.

The other side of desire is fear. As a survival strategy, fear is generated when we perceive our survival is threatened. There is nothing objective about this. Fear of rejection, failure, loss, criticism, even death, are all based on interpretation and perception. The ultimate fear, of course, is the fear of death, of dissolving back into source, of erasing the boundaries of our separateness. Thus all fear is based on ego's subliminally correct intuition that it is not really separate, and that it must continually scramble to shore up a sense of solidity in space and of endurance through time.

Fear also runs along a spectrum of mindbody states of worry-doubt-anxiety-repugnance-avoidance-dread-horror-paranoia-terror. We may notice that we often fear the mirror-opposite of what we desire or are attached to. If we desire approval or acclaim, we fear rejection; if we desire success, we fear failure or risk; if we hold on to power, we will avoid being controlled; if we desire winning, we are threatened by losing; if we are attached to life, we fear death. Understanding the play of this polarity helps to release our grip on fear. Ultimately, our freedom comes from seeing clearly through the fundamental interpretations that generate fear to begin with.

Desire and fear co-generate and sustain one another, arising interdependently as we forget our original nature. They then become the way the imagined incomplete self lives out its endlessly contradictory attempts to both sustain and heal its illusory incompletion and separation from the whole.

Our identification with the bodymind organism, and our attachment to its survival assumptions and strategies, is called "ego" in the Perennial Philosophy. While colloquially used in the West as arrogance or selfishness, here ego simply means the functioning that sustains the survival of the organism in which the Self has taken form. In essence it is the way the Self mediates through the world of embodiment. Yet when we identify with the I-thought, and attention gets caught in ego's web of belief and strategies, we forget our inherent, already existing wholeness; we then experience the suffering of separation and incompletion. Awareness becomes clouded by mind, and we become automatic unconscious victims of the struggle for survival. There is no real happiness, satisfaction, or love in the egoic domain, only clever counterfeits. Only when we turn to the source of ego do we find that what we have been seeking is already here and now.

This is the ultimate power of self-awareness. Awareness is pure, nonjudgmental observing. It just sees. As the context in which all thought takes place, awareness is free of the mind process. It is not caught up in the egoic drama. It witnesses mind. This awareness gives us a place to rest. It opens us to the peace of our being and to the unchanging happiness and fulfillment prior to desire and fear. Ultimately, awareness gives us freedom and choice.

When you are unconscious, you remain a mechanical victim of your own subliminal mental tendencies, painful habits, and counterproductive patterns. Heightened self-awareness reveals these habits and patterns, so that you can deal with them. You can accept them, let them go, or change them. Awareness gives you the choice to respond appropriately, to channel your power in the directions you choose.

When we are simply aware, simply witness the flow of mind and experience without identification or attachment, we come to intuit that this awareness itself is our true nature. Clear like space, unobstructed, at peace, you watch the dance of your own energy and consciousness. In this freedom, mind finds its rightful place as the instrument of Self and serves the organism to live out its destiny in the play of life.

In the clarity beyond mind and the I-thought we may discover the essence of leadership in our deepest being. Robert Rabbin has plumbed the depths of this mystery in his evocation of the Zen *koan*, in which the Master confronts the student with a riddle or question that has no conceptual answer, but is designed to shatter the mind's intellectual hold and reveal, in the silence of no-thought, intuitive knowing. "No one I know," writes Rabbin,

> has penetrated the koan of leadership. A koan is a riddle, the solution to which can only be found by going completely beyond all conditioning and thought. The solution originates from a place utterly free from image, belief, and concept. The mind that answers a koan is no mind at all; it is empty of all representation. Wrestling with the koan of leadership requires keen reflection and persistent inquiry. We must refine our awareness to have a chance of discovering what might be buried, a treasure, beneath the layers of conceptual thinking. An idea of leadership will always miss the mark; it is too slow and cumbersome; ideas cannot respond quickly enough to reality. This is why leadership is a koan. Any definition or formulation of leadership will miss the mark. Contemplate leadership as a means to become liberated from conditioning and thought. Then you will be qualified to be a leader.

Integrity

Integrity has long been considered one of the cardinal virtues of character in western culture. It is absolutely fundamental to the awakening of leadership and represents a perfect marriage of the spiritual and the practical.

Its original meaning from the Greek root is "whole, one, undivided." Integrity expresses the underlying wholeness of our true nature. The more we practice it, the more it strengthens our conscious experience of being whole. It is equally the means and the end, a source of effectiveness for both the self-aware individual and the conscious organization. It comes from the individual bottom line of ultimate being and serves the business bottom line of profit and strategic success. Integrity functions as both an individual and a collective quality. It is a true interface where the person and the organization meet, the very center of gravity for our ability to function effectively in life and work. Integrity is the supreme litmus test of authentic spirituality, be it organizational or personal. This fire of being true to yourself is both the core of personal strength and the ultimate driver of organizational resilience. Our challenge, then, is to live in integrity: to act self-referentially, consistent with who we are, what we stand for, and what we are here to do.

Integrity is based on a clear awareness of who we are and of our values, principles, and beliefs. There is a growing realization in business today that financial success can not be the only bottom line. As my online colleague, Barry Savage, put it: "Living by the [financial] bottom line is the cultural equivalent of living at the shallow end of the gene pool." There is a core of awakening leaders who believe that organizations must be *guided* by deep principles and moral, ethical considerations. Of course, business is clearly *driven* by market forces, and good intentions or positive values can't guarantee financial success.

Yet the question for reflective leaders remains: How do you ultimately define success? Is it just profit, or is it also the way you go about things and how you treat your people, your customers, your community and environment? "We need to argue for a new bottom line," Michael Lerner advises, "that judges productivity in terms of our ability to nurture ethically, spiritually, and ecologically sensitive human beings who are capable of sustaining long-term loving and committed relationships." A new bottom line is now emerging that integrates the quest for profit and living our deepest values.

Robert Haas, CEO of Levi Strauss, has taken his stand:

> Everyone looks at the wrong end of the telescope, as if profits drive the business. Financial reporting doesn't get to the real stuff—employee morale, turnover, consumer satisfaction, on-time delivery, consumer attitudes, perceptions of the brand, purchase intentions—that drives financial results. I believe that if you create an environment that your people identify with, that is responsive to their sense of values, justice, fairness, ethics, compassion, and appreciation, they will help you be successful. There's no guarantee—but I will stake my chips on this vision.

Another outstanding proponent of the power of values, James R. Houghton, former chairman of the board at Corning Incorporated, told his corporate management group in 1994:

> Values are not just nice concepts to write down or talk about. I believe that they are very powerful business tools. I wanted to make this point because some people think that these are "soft" issues. Some think that financial performance is for "real men" and that [the values of] Quality and The Individual are for "quiche-eaters." They feel that values are nice soft stuff, but only after you achieve superior financial performance can you afford to pursue these other values. Well, I say it just isn't so. You cannot get long-term, top-level, financial performance unless you deal with Values like Quality and The Individual. Performance follows these, it does not come first.

Under the guidance of Houghton and his successor Roger Ackerman, Corning has launched a comprehensive initiative to integrate lasting values into a set of specific real-time behaviors that can be evaluated regularly. This initiative provides the basis for a corporate operating environment intended to generate high performance and support the development of all their people.

For leaders committed to integrity, the first step is inner reflection to clarify your values. What do I deeply believe in? What do I just accept uncritically from my conditioning? How do I live my values in my work and leadership? What are the areas of incongruence and conflict with these values in my life? Is work a place where I can have consistency between my values and my behavior? Can I live out my integrity or right livelihood here? Must I change or even leave my work to remain in integrity? What is the meaning of my work in the context of my deepest purpose and commitments in life?

In daily work, integrity is expressed in speaking and acting consistently with what we stand for and what we are here to do. It is the fire of walking your talk and practicing what you preach. The workplace is literally held together by people giving and keeping their word: making promises, agreements, and commitments, delegating authority and taking responsibility, holding one another accountable, declaring visions and living out missions, engaging in open communication in an ongoing way.

This collective integrity channels enormous power. It drives high performance and ensures customer loyalty. It bestows a dignity and nobility of spirit which also engenders morale. It simplifies life and cuts through confusion. It is the bedrock of successful teams and the source of organizational cohesion and resilience. This is the collective word that generates the soul of the organization, its people bonded by trust, respect, and compassion for one another.

Integrity, the basis for trust in personal relationships, is no less important in the workplace. There has been such an erosion of trust in our organizations that people are tightly scrutinizing their leadership for the slightest breakdowns in integrity. The jaded view now is that leaders, especially highly visible ones, are guilty until proven innocent. And when the inevitable breakdowns occur, when they fail to live up to their word, it gives everybody the right to get even more cynical. While it is true that leadership must model integrity and be held fully accountable for any breakdowns, employees who simply seek to justify their cynicism with one more "I told you so, we can't trust them" are also showing some irresponsibility and lack of integrity.

Integrity is expressed as honesty, the willingness to speak one's truth, and give the appropriate constructive feedback to people in caring and supportive ways. Integrity is equally powerful in our choice to be silent when there is nothing productive to say. This honesty is the challenge we face if we are to create work and organizations that express our true nature. By opening and revealing ourselves we give everyone else an opportunity to do so as well. Mahatma Gandhi's belief in the power of the "truth force" (*satyagraha*) was clearly crucial to galvanizing mass support for India's independence. To take a stand is both scary and liberating. As Gandhi, Martin Luther King, and other leaders of great integrity have demonstrated, the energy of truth is contagious and catalyzes itself in others. While I do believe that "the truth shall set you free," how many of us are willing to take the risks of standing in our truth when it is most demanded? This openness begins as real vulnerability, but as we become accustomed to it, we find in it our strength and, ultimately, our invulnerability. In the long run, we come to realize that our only sanctuary is the truth and our commitment to live and be that truth.

Breakdowns in our integrity tend to be driven by the egoic survival strategies of fear and desire that protect or further our self-interest. They are rooted in and reinforce our belief in separation and incompletion. We sacrifice our integrity regularly out of our need for personal gain, ambition, profit, getting our way. This egoic focus is the primary cause of our suffering, and why the breakdowns in our integrity are so painful. They are denials of our always-already whole being and our unity with the rest of life. So we can see integrity as a way of being and acting that is not driven by survival, incompletion, or separation, but rather is both motivated by and serves our inner fulfillment as well as our unity with others.

There is a danger, however, in measuring integrity solely by behavior. Paradoxically, it is our own awareness of our consistency or inconsistency that is the true measure of our integrity. Knowing when we are out of integrity and coming back to it is also a function of integrity.

I see no point in succumbing to guilt. Usually, when the breakdowns and conflicts occur, guilt arises as a self-inflicted emotional punishment for our perceived transgression. My view is that the awareness of the behavior is enough, that guilt is self-indulgent suffering that does nothing for our integrity. Actually guilt reinforces the illusion of our smallness and incapacitates us from strong and effective action. Once we are aware of the transgression, all that is needed is to shift awareness back to our commitment and values, to our inherent whole being. Sometimes people need the intermediary steps of self-acceptance and self-forgiveness. Then it is essential to clean up any situational mess or consequences that may been created by the breakdown in integrity.

It is hard to speak of the fluid process of being true to oneself in purely black-and-white terms. I experience integrity as an ongoing meditation on who I am and a continual returning to myself. I see us coming in and out of integrity, an ongoing alternation of remembering and forgetting. It is a constant process of refocusing awareness and commitment whenever they are deflected. From this view, breakdowns in integrity don't invalidate our integrity as long as we are committed to returning to it continually.

This commitment strengthens our conscious grounding in our underlying Self, and allows behavior to flow more spontaneously from our whole being. In this spontaneity there is an automatic flow of action in which the individual becomes an instrument of the unfolding of the totality. Here inner wholeness and outer unity are one and the same.

As we live in integrity, we come to recognize that we are all participating in the interdependence of the wider whole. Our individual integral actions are the way the larger totality unfolds as a self-organizing system. In this age of networked connectivity, our integrity holographically reflects the underlying unity of existence. At a certain point we may come to realize that integrity is our best guide through the trackless unknown.

So much of integrity is expressed in speech. The word is an initial step in the creative process of translating idea into physical manifestation, the archetypal creative act itself. The Greek *logos* was incorporated by John in his Gospel as: "In the beginning was the Word, and the Word was with God, and the Word was God. He was with God in the beginning. Through him all things were made; without him nothing was made that had been made." (John 1:1–3). The Hindu version of this radical understanding of the process of creation is expressed in the ancient text, the Chandogya Upanisad: "All this phenomenal creation is strung together by the thread of speech." The classical Indian view affirms that the universe is being birthed by the original *Om*, the primal sound vibration or undertone of everything, the Self-Talk of the One Unmoving Mover, that radiates out and takes shape as the multiple worlds of existence.

These broad cosmologies are lived out in microcosm in the daily acts of speech by which leaders create the new. Each time we envision the big picture and spell it out in mission statements, strategies, goals, and objectives, we engage the process of creation. Each time you declare your truth and walk your talk, you are on the leading edge of the new. When we practice positive self-talk and empowering declarations to transform limiting beliefs and operating principles (see chapter six), we are literally engaged in the process of self-creation, cultivating a new way of becoming in the world. Your word is an expression of the Word. Your word expresses the universal creative power in everyday life and work. The individual leader's spoken acts of integrity—promises, agreements, declarations, visions, prophecies—are literally the microcosmic dimensions of the macro process of creation itself. This is the way the word becomes flesh, and the way the individual leader actively participates as an instrument of the whole.

In the Perennial Philosophy, it is said that when an individual realizes full self-awareness, that person's behavior flows spontaneously, guided intuitively by the deeper wisdom and energy that animates the universe itself. In this integrity, which is both an internal wholeness and an integration with the wider unity of life, there is no longer a distinction between individual self-interest and the good of the whole. Perhaps, in the same way, when a self-reflective organization lives out its collective integrity, it can generate appropriate forms and structures true to itself that enable it to evolve appropriately, in harmony with the ever-changing environment. Integrity, then, is the active demonstration of wholeness, a visible behavioral expression of our invisible being.

Courage

Because to live in integrity is to live at risk, authentic integrity is founded in courage. Courage is defined in the dictionary as mental or moral strength enabling one to venture, persevere, and withstand danger, fear, or difficulty firmly and resolutely. It is the firmness of spirit that faces danger or extreme difficulty without retreating.

In our mass-media, macho-oriented culture, courage is often portrayed simplistically as "no fear." But fear in some form is likely to arise when you take an unpopular stand, when you bet the farm and risk huge investments on a new product or strategy, when you say no to the boss or your customers, when you act decisively in the face of ambiguity, when you choose your values over short-term self-interest or your own personal survival. While fearlessness is, indeed, a condition of our ultimate being, we can not come to it by denying fear or trying an end run around it. In fact, courage is the willingness to go right through fear, to be fully open to it. The Tibetan Buddhist master Chögyam Trungpa Rinpoche, in his teachings on the sacred path of the warrior, noted: "In order to experience fearlessness, it is necessary to experience fear. The essence of cowardice is not acknowledging the reality of fear." Courage, then, is the willingness to face our fear and take the risks required by our integrity and deepest commitments.

It is significant that the word courage comes from the French *coeur* for heart and meant literally "more at heart." I relate this to the English word "core," the center or essence of something. So courage comes from your center, the core of power or energy at the heart of your being. Usually we use "mind" or "head" to relate to thought, and "heart" to refer to our feeling nature. In this sense true courage is the willingness to feel, to be fully present to the flow of sensation and emotion in your body.

Feelings are the forms your inherent strength takes. Your emotions are literally the motion of energy (e-motion) in your body. More specifically, an emotion is a thought coursing through your body, carried by neurophysiologic impulses and biochemical messages. Each emotion is the consequence of a certain interpretation. Fear is the result of an interpretation that your survival or well-being is threatened or at risk. This perception triggers the sensations we call fear.

The key to dealing with these emotions is to feel fully. When we feel fully, we give the emotion the opportunity to complete itself and dissipate. Emotions follow a simple basic law: if you feel them, they will pass. That is, if you feel them without clinging to your story or interpretation that generates them, then they come and go naturally. To feel an emotion is to accept it without judgment and experience it as pure sensation. When you do this, the emotion lives out its life span and disappears. If you don't face it, if you resist it, deny it, judge it, or repress it, it will stick around. It gets stored, either in the mind or the body as some form of stress or may show up eventually as illness.

To feel fully without judgment or interpretation opens us to experience sensation as it really is: pure energy. Fear, like other emotions, is a form our natural power or potentiality takes. When we experience it purely, we get the power of our true nature and discover how powerful we really are. We become alive *as* this energy, we are moved *by* this energy, filled *with* the vitality of our being. This is what the ancients called "enthusiasm," which literally meant to be filled with *theus,* that is, filled with God or the divine, the energy of the Self.

Courage, then, is the willingness to feel fully, to feel our emotions, our fear, our anger, our disappointments, our sadness. The choice to feel recreates within us a microcosm of the ancient science of alchemy—the process of transmuting base metals into gold—which was in essence a spiritual transformation. Within the very cells of our mindbody organism there occurs an alchemical transmutation of the base emotion of fear into the pure gold of courage. Wise leaders, then, not only understand that fear is the neurophysiological substrate and origin of courage, but also that situations of uncertainty and risk are the opportunities to manifest our integrity and strength. It is in this context that risk becomes exhilarating, the bubbling crucible in which courage is formed.

Courage is the willingness to go through your fears, feel them deeply, and act anyway. At first you come face to face with your vulnerability. As you become familiar with and trust the process of feeling, you find in it your strength and, ultimately, your invulnerability. If you truly understand that fear, indeed all your emotions, are simply modifications of the energy of the Self, you come to the threshold of fearlessness. When you realize that your underlying being is free and untouched by all the forms of its own energy, you will recognize fully that there is in fact nothing to fear. Once that radical interpretation shifts, you will indeed abide in the domain of fearlessness.

Of course, this doesn't mean being stupid or committing political suicide in your daily choices that involve risk. Sooner or later leaders develop the wisdom to distinguish when and when not to risk, to see under what circumstances it is intelligent or foolish. This situational savvy may guide you to recognize that courage may be required to see the reality of any situation just as it is, with no illusions or wishful thinking; or to take full responsibility for yourself, offering no excuses and assigning no blame to others; or when you have the opportunity to speak truth to those who hold power over you. This wisdom may reveal that it's prudent to play it safe when you're new in a situation and don't know enough of what's going on; or following periods of failure, extended risk, or expansion; or when you are operating in a low trust environment.

Here is a series of questions that help people identify their risks clearly enough to know when to be cautious and when to step forward courageously. Ask yourself: Where do I see myself most at risk, most challenged? What are the payoffs and costs in this situation? What am I unwilling to risk because the price is too high? What risks am I willing to take, and what would enable me to take those risks? What support do I need, and from whom, in order to take these risks and act decisively and effectively?

As Peter Block reminds us: "If our primary goal is to move up the organization, then in most cases we will act with caution. If, however, our primary commitment is to contribute, to be of service to our users, treat people well, and maintain our integrity, then we are doomed to a course of adventure, uncertainty, and risk. In fact, the very obstacles we fear are there to help us discover our own integrity. Only when we push hard against others and they resist do we really know where we stand."

Self-acceptance

It is often difficult to distinguish between the gold of true self-confidence required for courage and integrity, and the fool's gold of egotistical pride and arrogance. The leadership role can be a subtle trap that keeps people locked into the egoic mentality. It is easy to abuse the power and status of leadership—not only for personal gain in a material sense, but more subtly, to leverage that power to inflate one's sense of self.

If you have any doubt whatsoever about your inherent power or value, if you are attached to any limiting beliefs about who you are and what you are capable of, if you do not recognize that your full potential is already within you, then the tendency is to look outside yourself to seek the power, recognition, appreciation, and worth you don't think you have. In our intensely competitive, achievement-oriented, workaholic culture, it is the rule—at least for those of us subjected to traditional male conditioning—to try to measure and prove our sense of self through our position and accomplishment at work. Behind the ego battles in the workplace are the manifold manipulations to shore up a sense of self-worth and power.

Whatever subliminal self-doubt and lack of confidence we carry get a temporary fix by feeding on the power of the leader's position. As with any addiction, we feel all right as long as we are taking the drug. When the drug is withdrawn, we soon feel the crash of withdrawal—a sure sign we were not really well even with the drug. In this sense leadership is a temporary high, a drug of great addictive power. It is truly courageous not to use leadership in this way.

For the awakening leader committed to service and stewardship, the challenge is to come to an authentic sense of self that transcends the egoic trap. It is possible to serve the well-being of others without an agenda of self-aggrandizement. The most direct route is unconditional self-acceptance.

Self-acceptance is not to be confused with the egocentric narcissism that gets endorsed and encouraged in so much of the popular self-esteem literature. I want to describe a process that transcends ego while it, paradoxically, releases the unique potential coded within each of us for fulfillment and contribution in our work.

Self-acceptance calls for a simple, non-judgmental embrace of your whole being. You begin by accepting your mind and all your thoughts, your feelings and all your emotional reactions, and your behaviors, actions, and speech just as they are, not as you would wish them be to be. It is a gentle, loving, allowing of all your experience, regardless of the moods, feelings, and states you are going through. It is an acceptance of your being, no matter what your behavior.

To see yourself as you are calls for letting go of all judgments of yourself pro or con. Just let yourself be what you are, dimples and pimples, ups and downs, joys and breakdowns. Look into the mirror and see what's there. Embrace the whole package. What are you without qualifiers, without good and bad, likes and dislikes? This as-you-are is what Buddha called "suchness," that which is prior to judgment.

We can best appreciate our unconditioned nature by exploring the Biblical story of the Garden of Eden as a myth of consciousness. God had presented Adam with one commandment: "You must not eat from the tree of the knowledge of good or evil, for when you eat of it you will surely die." (Genesis 2:17). Adam, and shortly thereafter Eve, were free to live eternally in innocence: "The man and his wife were both naked and they felt no shame." (Genesis 2:25) The commandment was very clear: do not judge, do not bite into the distinction between good and evil. This is not your concern. Remain in innocent consciousness. This consciousness is your original nature which is eternal. This was the promise.

The judging quality of mind—eating the apple—divides the inherent perfection of creation into good and evil, right and wrong. The myth describes the origin of dualism, the separative mentality that divides the unity of existence into two, separates the individual from the whole, cleaves our original being into subject and object, creates the distance between the soul and God, between organism and environment.

This dualistic mentality literally casts us out of the garden of innocent consciousness. It casts us out of Paradise and into the world of suffering—the pain of childbirth and the "painful toil" of work and subsistence. It casts us out of the eternal now and into time, old age, and death. It is the fall into mind, into the suffering of ego's struggle to survive outside the garden of source consciousness.

In the dualistic mindset, opposites mutually generate and sustain each other. Once you believe in good, you have evil, and vice versa. Attachment to what you consider the positive creates the negative at the same time. Once you believe in high self-esteem you automatically create the possibility of low self-esteem. Self-criticism and arrogance feed one another. Once you set the standard of perfection, you are already falling short and are condemned to suffer the endless frustrations and disappointments of unattainable perfectionism. By seeking self-value or worth, you deny its existence already within you.

The point is to make no distinction whatsoever. The unitive consciousness sees the perfection of the whole. To not judge yourself is to see your own perfection. It is to see yourself, as Meister Eckhart said, through the eyes of God. God didn't make a mistake with you.

This is the paradox of unconditional self-acceptance. You accept all of yourself, even the unlikable, the painful, the violent, the ugly, the greedy aspects of you. This is what Jesus meant by forgiveness. You must forgive over and over each tendency as it arises because this forgiveness frees you from it. David Whyte poetically pointed out that full acceptance of your humanity allows you to see how all the parts of you fit together in a larger ecological whole which is complete as it is. You begin to see that even the so-called "flaws" —a category created by judgment—are part of your natural perfection.

Accepting everything opens your heart to a love that is infinitely greater than the narcissism and self-hatred generated by the dualistic mind. This love is all embracing, all-forgiving. It is the divine love which Jesus perfectly expressed and embodied. It's the merciful compassion by which the Self relates to itself. This love *is* the way, and it starts and ends with you.

Sometimes we fear that if we accept our upsets and breakdowns, we will be stuck with them. Actually, the reverse is more accurate. As the saying goes, "What you resist persists." That is, what you condemn or judge harshly about yourself will continue to repeat itself. It is easier to change an attitude, feeling, reaction, or behavior when you are willing to accept yourself for that experience. Acceptance, not rejection, is the most fertile and least painful basis for growth and change. It releases the energy for improvement and working on yourself.

Self-acceptance allows our natural commitment to excellence and total quality to surface without the tension inherent in the perfectionist drive. It resolves the workaholic stress of measuring our self-worth by our performance at work. This acceptance distinguishes the high performer from the perfectionist. We are free to pursue continuous improvement knowing that whatever we accomplish, be it success or failure, ceases to be a judgment on our nature. Instead, I can take the ultimate stand that I do the best I can and accept what I get. This takes courage in the face of relentless demands for peak performance.

Paradoxically, when you let yourself be, the inner resolve brings into action a mysterious power of its own that generates your best efforts. In acknowledging your underlying perfection, you are nurtured and empowered. All the energy that had been tied up in the tension of self-judgment is freed up to inspire and motivate you. Rather than a goal you seek, self-acceptance then becomes the constant companion and energizer of your journey of accomplishment in life.

The power of such acceptance is enormous. It literally heals suffering. It is especially in our upsets—our pain, breakdowns, anger, guilt, shame, sadness, mistakes—that we are most in need of acceptance rather than the self-blame, condemnation, or guilt we often apply to ourselves when we are down. Indeed, the place of pain within us is what most calls out for love and forgiveness. When you accept yourself in the midst of your pain and breakdown, you provide the healing needed, the most precious gift you have for yourself.

The voluminous literature on mindbody studies and psychoneuroimmunology testifies to the healing power of love. Bernie Siegel,

M.D.—the wise oncologist, surgeon, and professor at Yale University—has vividly argued that self-acceptance triggers neurotransmitters that strengthen the immune system: "I am convinced that unconditional love is the most powerful known stimulant of the immune system. If I told patients to raise their blood levels of immune globulins or killer T cells, no one would know how. But if I can teach them to love themselves and others fully, the same changes happen automatically. The truth is: love heals."

This love heals our sense of incompleteness. It is revealing how the words heal, whole, hale, and health all derive from the same Old English root *hal*. To heal is to awaken to the underlying wholeness. By putting us in touch with our prior fulfillment, it releases our limiting belief in being incomplete and the neediness which drives our desire. Desires and fears diminish naturally to more manageable proportions.

In realizing our own satisfaction, we can give freely to others without the need to manipulate for a return. When we are not needy, we can turn our attention from I-me-my-mine to focus on them. Service and stewardship are most successful when there is no personal agenda of acquisition. Then we are free to serve these ideals and to lead with the best interests of others at heart. This is the condition that fulfills the bodhisattva vow. This is the basis for the purity of leadership required by Nisargadatta Maharaj's bold declaration: "When more people come to know their real nature, their influence, however subtle, will prevail and the world's emotional atmosphere will sweeten up. When among the leaders appear some great in heart and mind and absolutely free from self-seeking, their impact will be enough to make the crudities and crimes of the present age impossible." Without the inner work, this might seem like pie-in-the-sky idealism.

This shift frees you from self-imprisonment in the struggle for survival and releases your energy to make your full contribution to work and life. All the energy that went into thinking you had to fight for survival gets freed up for greater vitality, joy, and enthusiasm for living out your destiny. You are able to take life lightly and play. You can finally let go of the ancient perfectionist pattern of looking at things around you and saying, "This isn't It." You get it that, whether you like it or not, you can choose to live in the stand that *This is it, this is my life*. You begin to understand what it means to be here now in the moment, to be satisfied and take pleasure in the simplicity of what is. You no longer postpone your right to enjoy being alive. You can celebrate every step along the way. This upbeat confidence and willingness to celebrate is a crucial source of inspiring leadership and workplace morale.

Self-acceptance brings about a fundamental shift in our sense of self and lays the groundwork for the humility essential to authentic spiritual life. We are humble when we embrace our humanity, foibles and all. Humility frees us from arrogance and the drive to inflate ourselves. It releases the need to be better than others, to puff ourselves up at others expense, to put people down in order to make us feel high. Nor is it about putting ourselves lower than others, bowing and scraping. This false humility is just more egoic posturing. Humility is the end of posturing and having to prove yourself.

This shift in self-concept is key to enlightened leadership. It frees you from the need to be right and in control, from abusing power and position, and feeding on admiration. It allows you to focus on others rather than yourself, to authentically empower others without your own power agenda interfering. You are able to give people credit, allow them to be visible and stand out, without fear of being overshadowed. It allows you to serve, as Robert Townsend, former head of Avis, described himself: as a waterboy for the team.

As the apocryphal Chinese sage Lao Tzu wrote in the sixth century BC:

> The best leader is one that the people are barely aware of.
> The next best is one who is loved and praised by the people.
> Next comes one who is feared.
> Worst is one who is despised.
>
> If the leader does not have enough faith in the people,
> They will not have faith in him.
>
> The best leader puts great value in words and says little
> So that when his work is finished
> The people all say, "We did it ourselves."

This transparency is an essential quality of the empowering leader—

transparent both in motivation and, ultimately, as a clear vessel of the light.

Finally, paradoxically, self-acceptance becomes self-transcendence.

As you fully accept the flow of mindbody experience as it is, a subtle shift in identification takes place. Instead of believing yourself to be the *content* of your experience, you realize that you are the *context* within which it is all occurring. You are the accepting context which allows the flow of thoughts, feelings, and actions to occur without attachment or judgment. You are the simple loving awareness which witnesses the egomind, and thus, is beyond it, untouched by experience. All states come and go, but you just are. This reveals your true nature which is pure being-awareness, which is fulfillment and unconditional love, which is selflessness. This is the return to the garden of innocent consciousness, which you discover has always been here, behind mind, awaiting your acceptance. Neither a place in time nor a state of mind, it is your very nature.

In this realization you can finally understand the Biblical injunction to love thy neighbor as thyself. That is, you can only authentically love your neighbor if you love yourself in this way. Your ability to accept yourself frees up your ability to love others. When your heart is open to yourself, it opens naturally to others and the dualistic boundaries dividing self and other dissolve. You can experience your relatedness with all beings and allow your innate compassion and love to flow out effortlessly to them.

The Heart of Compassion: Sharing the Gift of Love

Compassion is a fundamental aspect of most spiritual traditions. In the paradox of spiritual practice, compassion is both an approach to our true nature and an expression of it. The Dalai Lama, an authentic exemplar of Buddhist compassion, points out that there can be no wisdom without compassion. Unitive insight gives birth to compassion, which then must accompany the sword of wisdom. In the Biblical tradition, God *is* love, and the essence of Christianity which Jesus fully embodied is the practice of love.

Leadership is an extraordinary opportunity for expressing our caring for others. I have been asking my clients for years if it is possible to express love and compassion in the workplace, and what would it look like if they did. With the increasing stress, overwork, mistrust, and low morale at work today, it seems not only appropriate but necessary to touch this suffering. The call of Zen Master Taisen Deshimaru, who eloquently describes the commitment of the bodhisattva, is just as relevant to the awakening leader:

> Do not remain on the summit of the mountain of solitude.
> Paddling muddy water by the landing-stage,
> The highest spirit of compassion penetrates the three worlds.
> You must be content to be a ferryman on the sea of sufferings.

James Autry, another poet and a former president of the Meredith Corporation, lyrically invokes the essence of the compassionate leader's role: "Listen. In every office you hear the threads of love and joy and fear and guilt, the cries for celebration and reassurance and somehow you know that connecting those threads is what you are supposed to do and business takes care of itself."

In the space of love business can indeed take care of itself. Like gravity, the force of attraction that holds the heavenly bodies together, love is the cohesive force that joins people in the conscious organization. Given the hardball atmosphere in most workplaces, it is a risky, vulnerable stand for leaders to express their love openly and encourage it in others. One of the most powerful examples is Herb Kelleher, president of Southwest Airlines, who unabashedly professes his love for his employees in the most flamboyant ways and regularly bestows his "Heroes of the Heart" award for outstanding customer service. Their joy and love is palpable on their flights. It is no accident that this company consistently ranks at the top of the list for customer service among U.S. airlines.

The love of the awakened leader is expressed in valuing each individual, their unique potential and contribution. As the emotional basis for empowerment and partnership efforts, love means believing in people and holding them as able. This often requires the x-ray vision to see through peoples' surface reservations about their own limitations to the deeper promise. I remember very clearly my sixth-grade teacher, Mr. Lindgren. In his class I literally felt more able and better about myself. On the playground I could run faster and was a better athlete when he was our football coach. When Mr. Lindgren looked at us, he didn't see just a bunch of fidgety sixth-graders with their lunch boxes. He saw future leaders, politicians, professionals, athletes. He believed in us and we could feel it subliminally. Empowering leaders literally generate a field of possibility around them. When you enter it, you are energized and in touch with your potential and what is possible for you. It ignites your deepest aspirations and clarifies your own inarticulate dreams.

This love is also expressed in leaders' commitment to the success and well-being of their people. They want their people to do well and they provide the conditions and resources for that to happen. It is quite a challenge to honestly want others to succeed. To do so, we must have already worked through our own ambition and redefined our self-interest so that we are not competitive with or feel threatened by the live wires around us. This is the hallmark of a great master: "You will do even greater things than I." For the authentic teacher, there is joy in watching your student or protegé go beyond you. Their success is your success.

Rather than viewing this as some passive sacrifice of our self-interest, I see it as expanding our self-interest to embrace the success and well-being of others. One's sense of self expands to include what we take full responsibility for, what we are truly committed to. Our identity may expand to include a gender group, a racial, ethnic, or religious group, the species, all of nature. For leaders committed to the well-being of their people, their identity expands to embrace their staff, the wider team or organization. When we have a global vision and are committed to the well-being of the planet, our sense of self can be truly planetary, embracing all of humanity and nature. The full expansion our self-interest takes in the well-being of the whole.

For the mature leader, love shows up in the commitment to grow and develop people through coaching and mentoring. This involves a real-time involvement in ongoing relationship and communication, a choice to give of one's time and energy for others. I am continually impressed with how much attention the conscientious managers I coach devote to performance reviews, one-on-one coaching, and appropriate constructive and appreciative feedback for their employees. This is a major investment that expresses authentic caring for people.

Coaching and mentoring gives leaders a context to share their wisdom in ways that support others. As we mature in leadership we can take on the role of elders. In a society that worships youth and the new, that has such a fear and denial of death, a suspicion of aging, and an unwillingness to be bothered by our aging parents, we tend to devalue the wisdom of experience. We shunt our elders off to retirement condominiums and shuffleboard courts, or by neglect condemn them to roam the interstates in their RV's. With the demographics of rapid aging in our society, it is clearly time to recognize the wisdom of age and listen to our elders. Leadership is a domain in which to pass on the legacy of experience, and make the transmission of wisdom to the next generation.

One of the most extraordinary acts of compassion by corporate leadership was by Aaron Feuerstein, the owner of Malden Mills, producer of the popular Polartec fleece used in winter wear. In December 1995 an explosion and fire injured 33 workers, destroyed three factory buildings, and threw 1400 employees out of work for what threatened to be an indefinite period. The night of the fire, Feuerstein showed up and declared "with God's help we will overcome." He gave each employee their paycheck plus a $275 Christmas bonus, as well as coupons for food at the local grocery store. Three days later he guaranteed everyone's salaries for another thirty days and paid their health insurance premiums for the next three months, declaring that within ninety days they would be fully operational again. A month later Feuerstein announced he would continue paying workers for another month. Repairs and new buildings were soon completed and the company got back in operation on schedule.

Aaron Feuerstein's loving commitment to his employees and the local community was not a one-shot deal. Over the years he has helped many employees buy houses, pay for funerals, and send their kids to college. When questioned on his motives and why he didn't just collect the insurance and move on, Feuerstein, a Jew who quotes Hillel and Shakespeare, commented simply: "I thought rebuilding was the right thing to do and what I had to do. And then some people thought

I did such a saintly thing. I did a normal thing." This is only normal for a man of heart who cares about people and his community.

At work, compassion can show up in simple ways. I think of it as real respect for the inherent equality and dignity of our co-workers, a sensitivity to their needs, issues, and experiences. It is a wholehearted commitment to valuing and celebrating diversity, to not be threatened by differences but to welcome and incorporate them into the way we work. It is the willingness to understand people, put ourselves empathetically in their shoes, let them be who they are and go through their ups and downs. We express our compassion in listening to one another, even if we don't agree, in respectfully telling someone the truth you believe they need to hear, and giving constructive feedback in a caring and supportive way rather than just criticizing. Compassion understands that appreciation and positive feedback are deeply nurturing and empowering to people. It is the choice to support risk-taking and reward it whether it succeeds or not, to not claim to be right all the time, and to deal supportively with the inevitable mistakes, errors, and failures that occur daily. It is needed when leaders, who have made the difficult decision to downsize, personally discuss their misgivings or emotions with those affected, and offer healing interventions for everyone in the organization going through rapid change.

Compassion is not just the ability to put oneself in the other's place and be sensitive to their experience. It is not just imagining, "There but for the grace of God go I" or, as the Native Americans say, "Don't judge anyone till you've walked a mile in their moccasins." It is above all the willingness to feel with others, from the Latin *com* + *patio*, meaning literally to suffer with or bear with.

Ironically, once you choose the spiritual life, you see even more clearly that the world is full of suffering and cynicism. Compassion involves the willingness to directly face the suffering of others and respond from the heart. The heart of compassion is a vast space of tenderness within which we can allow everything to exist. We usually inure ourselves to pain and so will not open the tender heart to suffering, ours or another's. Our fear of vulnerability itself holds us back. If we can allow ourselves to be vulnerable without the usual armor, we can feel ourselves, feel the world, and open the heart of mercy to those around us. Like courage, compassion is only experienced through the fire of feeling.

Opening our deepest feeling core to others allows us to see, in the unity of existence, our own true face in all beings. Mother Teresa said that she saw "Christ in his most distressing disguise" in every leper and suffering soul she met. In this unitive vision, you know that everyone is a form of you, that all of us are individuated expressions of the same all-pervading presence and source. We are not just brothers and sisters, but literally members of one body.

When we see everyone as our own wider Self, the natural and appropriate response is compassion. As the thumb spontaneously, compassionately helps the finger, so does one conscious expression of the Self touch another. It is not some forced service to the "other," but the very love that you have for yourself. Compassion is the feeling tone of unity, the intuitive, emotional relationship the Self has with itself. "Love the world as your own self," wrote Lao Tzu, "then you can truly care for all things."

The way of compassion is a bittersweet walk. Ram Dass has captured the paradoxical and mysterious nature of compassion in action: "It accepts that everything is happening exactly as it should, and it works with a full-hearted commitment to change. It sets goals but knows that the process is all there is. It is joyful in the midst of suffering and hopeful in the face of overwhelming odds. It is simple in a world of complexity and confusion. It is done for others, but it nurtures the self. It shields in order to be strong. It intends to eliminate suffering, knowing that suffering is limitless. It is action arising out of emptiness."

Mother Teresa echoed the same mystery when, sending her missionaries of charity out to work with the poor and suffering, she reminded all of us, "Never let anything so fill you with sorrow as to make you forget the joy of Christ Risen." The vow of the bodhisattva is to live in the midst of suffering and shine your light anyway, knowing indeed that the light is always here, just as the sky is always present no matter how cloudy it appears. The strength to live with an open heart and share the bright vision of possibility with people is fed by this realization that there is, in truth, no dilemma, despite all appearances to the contrary. As the great Sufi poet-saint Rumi beckoned: "Come, come, whoever you are, this caravan has no despair." Though you may wander away a thousand times, you only need turn your face toward love once again to be welcomed home. When you face the sun the shadows are behind you.

V

MARK OF COURAGEOUS LEADERSHIP

The qualities of leadership described in chapter four are developed in the real-time process of working on oneself in the mundane circumstances of everyday work life. It is tempting to think—or hope—that awakening and mastery are cultivated by some painless or lofty revelation, rather than by facing the unglamorous challenges of the day-to-day management process—dealing with your staff and boss, with budgets, deadlines, performance reviews, troubled employees, conflicted departments, and shifting customer needs. God, it is said, is in the details. Buddhism's classic image of enlightenment is a lotus blooming in the muddy waters of ordinary life.

I want to tell the story of a manager who turned severe demands into an opportunity for developing greater self-awareness, courage, integrity, and self-acceptance as a leader. It shows clearly some of the difficult, often emotional experience on the journey of mastery. The story is specially significant to me because it was my first in-depth experience with coaching someone through a 360-degree feedback process—a process I have subsequently used in different formats to support dozens of leaders to grow. I have been deeply impressed with how this powerful process provides a simple and effective method for developing the self-knowledge at the heart of courageous leadership.

A Novel Experiment

I first met Mark in December 1995 in preparation for the "Feedback for High Performance" workshops I was presenting for his company's research and development organization. In the midst of large scale reorganization and an accelerated drive to compete in the rapidly expanding global opto-electronics and telecommunications market, the corporation was committed to creating an open, high-performance culture that could tap the full creative potential of all its members.

I was being given a specific opportunity to support the growth of a conscious organization by facilitating the flow of intelligent feedback among its members. The science and technology division was made up of talented, often brilliant professionals and experts—people with much to contribute to one another if they could learn appropriate methods and skills for communicating honestly about performance issues. The division's Human Resource Director felt that sessions on constructive and appreciative feedback would develop interpersonal skills essential to a free exchange of ideas among the scientists, technicians, engineers, and developers involved. She had arranged for me to meet individually with department managers to brief them on the upcoming seminars and discuss issues specific to each of their departments.

Mark is a bright, soft-spoken, and sincere scientist-manager. At the time, he had four years' experience in the company's managerial ranks. He had been brought up from one of the business groups less than two years earlier to manage a new research and development department that had been pieced together in the re-engineering effort.

In our first meeting, Mark spoke of the difficulties he faced creating a united department from three previously separate groups of engineers, research scientists, and product development specialists. Each of these groups valued their autonomy and did not relish being merged with the others. If that wasn't challenging enough, Mark was a geochemist who found himself managing a group of engineers, research chemists, and technicians—most of whom knew more about the scientific specialization of the department than he did and who doubted that he had the expertise to manage their projects or appreciate the detail of their work. In fact Mark had been hired with the confidential understanding that he might be replaced when an expert in the department's specialization was found. In addition, there were a few ongoing interpersonal conflicts among departmental members that further complicated an already difficult situation.

The recent corporate Climate Survey, a written instrument quoting the anonymous comments of members of Mark's department, had come back with a number of reservations about his managerial abilities and interpersonal skills. Concerned and surprised with this feedback, Mark met with me and the division's human resource specialist Sherry, a savvy, street-smart professional with a solid knowledge of the departmental situation and the players involved. The three of us planned a strategy for Mark to better understand the issues, with the goal of improving himself as manager and addressing the underlying problems of the department.

It was obvious we would have to go deeper than the anonymous written feedback. Together we devised a bold plan which would put into direct action the guidelines for constructive feedback we had covered in my seminars. No more workshop role-play. This would be face-to-face discussions about real issues, perceptions, and feelings. It was a practical opportunity for the department to implement the corporate initiative toward a more open, engaging culture based on frank dialogue and honest feedback.

We carefully set up a two-track system. In the first, Mark would get direct feedback from ten members he selected from his department. These people would meet individually one-on-one with him in private, confidential sessions that I would facilitate. Mark selected individuals whom he felt would be candid with him. A few of these people were his major nemeses, outspoken people who had serious reservations about his performance as a manager. They had had emotional encounters with him. Some of them claimed they could not work with him. These were not cream puffs.

We arranged that each of the ten department members would first attend a prep session with Sherry and me. There we would lay out ground rules for the feedback session and discuss the specific issues they had with Mark and the department. We wanted them to be fully prepared to give direct, no-holds-barred feedback, within the guidelines established in the seminar. We were also careful to assure them that there would be no personal retaliation—that Mark was serious about listening to what they had to say, and would not hold it against them.

While the initial focus was on Mark's performance as a manager, we wanted to avoid a "get-Mark" mentality. We expanded the feedback to include each individual's and the department's collective responsibility for the problems discussed. Mark was only one player in a complex pattern of issues rooted in many causes. While Mark was willing to own his piece, we wanted each person to take full responsibility for their feedback and for their role in any of the departmental issues. It is easy in an anonymous written instrument like the Climate Survey to give unthought-out or irresponsible critical feedback. In the one-on-one sessions, people were expected to take ownership of their views, support them by citing specific behaviors, events, and impacts, and come up with positive suggestions for change—not only for Mark, but also for themselves and the department.

On a parallel track, we planned that I would meet concurrently with Mark in a series of one-on-one coaching sessions that would focus on his personal and professional development and help him digest the feedback he was getting. We established an easy rapport and a mutual understanding that circumstances such as these are vivid opportunities for greater inner growth and self-awareness. Mark was eager to explore the personal roots of his managerial issues and was committed to a process of intensive transformation as an individual and a manager.

We also scheduled a final summary session with the ten participants to take place at the end of the feedback sessions. This would be an informal celebration and dinner meeting, in which Mark would summarize the feedback he heard, discuss his personal commitments to change, and lay out proposed action steps for the department.

Heading for White Water

This "novel experiment," as Mark called it, turned into a remarkable act of courage in the midst of a very polite corporate culture where most of the managers would not consider opening themselves to such an extent with their staff or peers. They were reluctant enough just to participate in the corporate mandate requiring them to get indirect, anonymous written feedback, which they could then read and consider in privacy. A few might go to the Center for Creative Leadership or some other intensive leadership development program, where they would get confrontive feedback from trained facilitators. But to sit down one-on-one with the people you manage daily, listen to their feedback on your performance as their manager, and actually dialogue on the issues until there is understanding and commitment to action— that is courageous leadership.

Obviously for Mark, it was a choice for growth over self-protection, driven by his own realization that he had to take the bull by the horns and proactively develop his managerial and interpersonal skills. Besides, his boss had just given him his annual performance review. He said that Mark lacked assertiveness and wasn't pushing his staff hard enough. While Mark had the full support of his boss, it was also clear he had better seize this opportunity now to work on both himself and the department.

I was impressed with Mark's determination to walk directly into this fire. As a consultant I definitely appreciate the opportunity to work with someone so committed to change, and to have this degree of permission to foster both the personal and organizational dimensions of transformation. I saw him modeling the open, risk-taking spirit and commitment to ongoing learning that is the essential basis of personal mastery and leadership.

In one of our first personal coaching sessions, Mark told me of his love of white water rapids—which he had done many times while boating in the Grand Canyon. He noted that this feedback program was like going into white water. You prepare for it as best you can. You can get out of the boat and look over the rapids as much as you want. Once you get back in the boat and push off, he knew from experience, there is no going back. The same skills that get you through white water get you through the interpersonal and organizational turbulence: alertness, expecting the unexpected, willingness to take a hit, ability to respond quickly to new input, sensing the hidden depths and rocks, agility with shifting weight, balance, and confidence in your ability to handle it. Yet no matter how well you have prepared, once you are in the midst of it, you have to take what comes and trust. I could feel all of that, including the uncomfortable blend of apprehension, uncertainty, and quiet resolve that Mark was feeling as we prepared to face the beast head-on.

Inner Work

As we got ready for the feedback meetings, Mark and I began weekly individual coaching sessions. I introduced him to fundamental principles and guidelines for developing greater understanding of himself. We focused initially on exploring his non-assertiveness: describing the behaviors, looking at the deep assumptions underlying his behavior, the payoffs that held these assumptions in place, and the costs to him and others associated with his non-assertiveness. As we developed his self-awareness, it became clear that lifetime patterns of belief and self-image were blocking his effectiveness as a manager—both the way he related to his staff and how he related to his boss. At a certain point in our growth, we come to realize that professional development requires an inner transformation of basic operating assumptions and self-image: Mark had reached that point.

He saw that the situation was calling for him to grow from his original focus as scientist-businessman to a wider vision of himself as a people-oriented manager. This new vision would both include and transcend his old orientation and require him to cultivate a new set of interpersonal qualities and behaviors. We focused on developing the vision and goals for a new way of being as manager. He began practicing an inner technology of transformation, working with positive self-talk and visualization techniques, following the guidelines detailed in chapter six below.

Mark showed an earnest enthusiasm for getting greater insight into himself. He is basically introspective and has a longtime practice of recording his self-reflections in leather-bound manuscript books. I was pleased that he was already familiar with the internal orientation needed to work on himself effectively. Mark's preparation and quiet resolve to go through with it were especially important, for the feedback sessions were about to open his eyes to the magnitude of the changes required of him.

Feedback, the Breakfast of Champions

Sherry and I met individually with each participant to prep them for the feedback process. After discussing the purpose and format of the upcoming one-on-one sessions, we shared with each participant a list of issues Mark considered he needed to improve, based on the Climate Survey and informal feedback he had heard over time. He was concerned about his communication with the department: Was it too much, too little? Did they feel in the dark? Was his style too stiff? Not assertive enough? He had begun to suspect that they didn't feel valued or adequately recognized by him. Mark's other major concern was that he was not providing a proper strategic framework for the department. Did they have a secure sense of where they were going and how it all fit together?

The prep sessions were extremely important for all of us in getting ready for the feedback, especially as it became obvious there was strong dissatisfaction with Mark's performance as a manager. I was surprised at the strength of the emotional charge some of the department members were carrying toward him. The majority answered most of Mark's management-issue questions in the negative. For some it was an affront to not be listened to, to feel undervalued, to have their advice ignored or summarily dismissed. The litany of complaints came out: Mark valued Ph.D.'s over the rest, favored scientists over engineers, didn't listen well or take advice, didn't express appreciation, micromanaged, didn't seem to trust people to make decisions, didn't explain his decisions.

It was also clear that people were willing to blame Mark for issues he had nothing to do with. It is typical for employees to blame management rather than take personal responsibility for their role in their own upsets, their passivity in improving the situation, or their self-interested manipulations and concerns. Some of the participants did see that Mark had inherited a virtually "unmanageable department," as one of them called it, which was enmeshed in a complicated net of interpersonal conflicts and power politics. They expressed a greater appreciation of Mark's situation and his ability to handle it. Others were very positive and experienced no problems in their relationships with Mark.

All the participants showed some apprehension about participating in direct feedback with their manager. But as we went though the prep sessions we noted some relaxation of tension as they saw they would have an opportunity to be heard in a safe setting. Only one individual, who had already left the department, opted out of the process. The others seemed ready, if not eager, to sit down with their boss.

The direct one-on-one feedback sessions with Mark and each of the participants flowed smoothly over a condensed two-week period. With the participants prepped, and Mark briefed on the issues, they had extremely heartfelt meetings that directly confronted realities in a productive way. We framed the conversation as an opportunity for dialogue not only on Mark's role, but on how everyone could take greater responsibility for improving the department. We saw it as an opportunity for people to practice the skills required for the company's new corporate operating environment, which encouraged greater openness and engagement among people. The dialogue was structured as comment and response on a list of issues raised in the prep sessions. Each person had an opportunity to give their feedback, respond to the other, clarify misunderstandings, and make requests of one another for future actions and support.

When people are properly prepared to sit down face to face as fellow human beings, they are more willing to be responsible for what they say and to be more understanding of one another. While they didn't hold back their punches, there was a greater sense of appreciation and even compassion for each other. Direct person-to-person communication opens up a space that allows the truth to come through and creates a human bond between the individuals that would not be there if this were just a written procedure. I was impressed with the honesty and bravery of all the parties going through the process.

Absorbing the Blow

After the first two one-on-one dialogues, Mark was doing well. He was facing the challenge and responding well to the feedback. During the next few sessions, as some of the more difficult feedback came through, the brunt of it started to hit him. In one debriefing session, Mark confided, "It's a lot worse than I thought it would be." It was clear that he was only then fully realizing the way some people experienced him. This was not an easy recognition. It gave Mark some troubled nights and plenty of food for thought. I call it "doing your laundry," when you painfully face your difficult or ineffective tendencies and see vividly their effects in your life.

In our coaching sessions mid-way through the feedback process, I was impressed with how well Mark absorbed the input and kept his resolve to carry on. In fact the more confrontive the feedback, the more he seemed willing to use it as compost for his self-knowledge and personal-professional growth.

Mark had reached a crucial point in the emergence of greater self-awareness. It takes courage and commitment to look unflinchingly at oneself, just as it calls for authentic integrity and responsibility to accept the feedback without caving in to blaming and "shooting the messenger." It also takes a stable self-acceptance to receive such a litany of complaints about oneself without floundering in guilt and self-blame. Mark not only hung in there gamely, he proactively began to chart new changes for himself and the department.

He made the clear commitment to become "a manager of all the people." This was a fundamental shift in Mark's self-image as a leader. He was moving further away from the egoic focus on "I" to a wider embrace of others' concerns and well-being. We discussed how this was a significant step in his transition from scientist to manager, and that it would have profound implications for his career and personal life as will.

In practice this meant becoming more interpersonally skillful and sensitive to others, willing to appreciate and support his people fairly, and acting more as a coach focused on their well-being, development, and empowerment. We emphasized the inner techniques necessary to initiate this shift, and began working more intensely on affirming, envisioning and directing his energy in his chosen direction. He needed to find the subtle balance between assertiveness and sensitivity, to bring forth his strength and yet be there to serve, support and empower his people.

It was to Mark's credit that he was also beginning to consider, while we were at the most painful point of the feedback process, how to use this information for positive change in the department. We discussed how we would monitor the process after we finished the interviews and make sure it would continue to work. He wanted to encourage everyone to continue to give him direct feedback. Mark also began organizing all the feedback he was receiving into a wide range of topics, from which to put together specific action plans.

After this turning point, Mark began showing greater energy, more insight and confidence. He actually began implementing changes right then. He ended the practice of having two separate department meetings—one for direct reports, the other for the rest of the department. To encourage unity and show he valued everyone equally, he created one integrated meeting.

After three more feedback sessions, Mark was showing great strength and commitment. He was on a roll with a glint in his eye as he started talking about getting feedback from all his management colleagues as well. I laughed as I asked him if he hadn't had enough feedback yet. He was clearly moving into the high performance mentality now, seeking out feedback, literally being empowered by it. He had dealt with fear and upset and was using it as rich manure for the coming harvest. I liked the process I saw happening. Some of the feedback had been very tough, and here he was asking for more. Definitely a man on a mission.

Mark's session with Bob was especially important. Bob was a highly respected engineer, an old pro who had been in the company twenty-nine years and probably could have been selected for the department manager's job had he wanted it. Bob was the leader of a highly visible, mission-critical development project, and was instrumental in the success of the whole department. He did not welcome having his engineering group come under the management of a research specialist such as Mark. He had a hard time with Mark's attempt to manage him, feeling that Mark didn't trust him and wouldn't empower him to run his own ship.

In their one-on-one session, they had a very frank discussion. Bob was upfront with his feedback and gave Mark valuable tips on motivational leadership and team-building. We elicited his willingness to support Mark, to be a mentor for him during the remaining two years before his retirement. We spoke of letting go of old attitudes, especially his feeling of not being trusted or valued by Mark. While he admitted it might not be easy, he was willing to try.

The session with Bob, and a few others with key individuals, were clear breakthroughs in long-standing problematic relationships and issues in the department. It felt like the clouds were parting to reveal some blue sky in which everyone could breathe a bit more easily and begin to work together with greater harmony and understanding.

Launching the Transformation

When we finished the feedback sessions, Mark transferred the suggested actions and requests we had collected onto Post-its and arranged them in categories on a poster-board. There in front of us, filling half his office wall, emerged a comprehensive plan for personal and departmental transformation. He divided the results into proposed changes for himself individually and for the department collectively.

Mark targeted an array of interpersonal behaviors and attitudes that he individually would be committed to developing:

- Consult before deciding
- Listen, give clear feedback, acknowledge understanding, and explain his decisions
- Value and appreciate before analysis of business application
- Build relationships, be visible and available to people, visit labs and different work sites more frequently

To build relationships and expand his coaching role, Mark planned a comprehensive schedule of one-on-one meetings over the course of the year with everyone in the department. He wanted to establish a personal relationship and open communication with each individual, get to know each of them, provide coaching on their personal growth and career development, and work out a clear contract between himself and them on how they could work together with mutual responsibility to promote positive change in the department.

For the department as a whole, Mark was committed to:

- Lead and articulate a strategic vision with group consensus
- Support his staff and run interference for them in the company
- Learn more about the department's scientific specialization
- Plan and conduct the expansion of department hiring
- Hold fully inclusive monthly meetings with a participatory agenda
- Have team-building sessions to unify the department
- Value all the people and give recognition at all levels

Mark then invited all the feedback participants to a final dinner meeting in which he would present the results of the process. In his memo announcing the meeting he noted:

> The feedback sessions we've had together have been for me an intense, at times difficult, but enormously rewarding experience. I'm using this experience as the basis for change for a number of my own behaviors and practices as well as for changes I will ask of the department.

Mark showed great energy and enthusiasm in preparing for the final meeting with the feedback people. Having been through the fire, he was now emboldened to stand before them assertively, with clear ideas about how he was changing and how the department needed to take responsibility to change as well. Everyone would be called to higher performance and teamwork.

The dinner meeting was a first-class affair from start to finish. Held in a private dining room in the elegant new company headquarters, it was both a reward and celebration for the intensity everyone had gone through. The gathering had an informal, intimate feel to it. Mark was open and personable as he described the need for change, summarized the feedback he received from everyone, and announced the action steps and commitments he would make personally. He made requests for support and commitment from the participants and invited them to be a vanguard of support to move the whole department toward greater unity and teamwork.

It was a warm, open session with all but one of the participants engaged and supportive. We wrapped up the dinner with a group visualization of the department functioning at optimal trust, openness, and unity, which brought out some inspired comments. Mark also arranged for tasteful gifts for the participants. People were moved by the whole process and pleased that their feedback had been heard and that we were moving toward implementation.

Two weeks later, Mark presented the results of his feedback experience to the whole department—who had been hearing informally about the process through the grapevine. It started slow and stiff, perhaps because some of those not involved in the original feedback process were apprehensive that they might have to go through one-on-one feedback too. Folks warmed up and relaxed as the session unfolded and they realized the depth of Mark's commitment to change and his positive vision of a high-morale, unified, team approach. He let them know it was time to let go of the past. He invited them to give up their cynicism, make a commitment to support change, and become proactive in creating the new department. There was a sincere, intelligent discussion, with realistic concerns expressed but no real opposition. People were relieved that the veil of apathy and mistrust was being lowered and we were moving toward positive solutions. In that spirit, the whole department got involved in planning a two-day overnight team-building retreat that I would facilitate for them the following month.

The next week Mark took everyone on an all-day excursion boat ride down the Erie Canal with catered lunch, refreshments, and gifts. It was a playful, relaxing day spent together, with one short award process in the middle of the trip to recognize a number of people for their contributions to the department. It was good to see the social bonding taking place among the disparate groups in the department, and useful for me to get to know more of them in preparation for the upcoming retreat.

With a Little Help from My Friends

Just as we were completing the verbal feedback process, the company announced that all managers were expected to participate in an extensive 360-degree written feedback exercise to assess and promote positive leadership behavior. I was struck by how eager Mark was to get feedback from his peers, as well as from other members of the department who hadn't participated in the first round. When I suggested he might have had enough input already, he said no, he expected to get a different kind of information on different topics. Not only that, he suggested that if the written responses from his peers weren't clear enough, perhaps we could sit down with them and clear up it up verbally. Mark was literally thriving on feedback now and enthused about involving his fellow managers in supporting his growth and learning.

He was feeling empowered as a member of the division's leadership team, consisting of his fellow technology and business managers. He had been sharing his feedback experience with some of the other managers, many of whom were incredulous that he actually went through it voluntarily. Ironically, now that they were all involved in the written 360-degree process, Mark was pleased that he had already done the hard face-to-face work. He and his department were ahead of the curve in opening up authentic feedback and beginning to implement the new corporate operating environment.

We began receiving some early indications of the positive effects of the process on the way people in the department saw Mark. The next Climate Survey for the department was taken, coincidentally, just after the feedback process was completed. Mark scored higher on his interpersonal skills, with favorable ratings for his openness, engaging, coaching and listening skills. The department showed a greater overall satisfaction with Mark. It is fascinating how the consciousness of the group was changing in response to the openness and good intentions of the people involved. The very process of communicating honestly with one another brought a shift in perception.

Going Deeper into Consciousness

As we were finishing up a personal coaching session one day Mark mentioned he had just reread Kerouac's *The Dharma Bums*. It was a welcome opening for us to carry our conversation to deeper dimensions of the experience he and the department were going through. We talked about Zen, about being fully awake in the moment and how powerful this practice is in our lives and work. Mark had practiced meditation and referred to moments in whitewater and rock climbing as experiences of expanded awareness and unity with nature. I was enthused to discover this deeper connection with Mark, and to find a way to relate my lifelong involvement in meditation and the Perennial Philosophy to the specific work we were doing. My work was becoming increasingly devoted to supporting people in the corporate world to become more conscious and to shape their work and organizations from this awareness.

In subsequent meetings we might take short meditation breaks. We spoke of pure awareness in which the sense of separation dissolves into the flow and there is a spontaneous experience of team unity, of the one mind interacting in perfect harmony. We explored the image of the wave and the ocean and how there is no real separation between the individual mind and the ground of consciousness which is our common source and essence. We discussed the practical implications of this unitive awareness in Phil Jackson's book, *Sacred Hoops*, a fascinating description of how Jackson, coach of the Chicago Bulls, gradually introduced meditation, compassion, and unity consciousness into team training that helped the '96 Bulls become one of the greatest teams in basketball history.

We began to see the underlying connections between Mark becoming more conscious as a leader, the department becoming more conscious as a team, and the whole corporation becoming a more aware organization committed to open communication. We applied an insight of the whole-systems approach: As self-organizing systems evolve to greater complexity, an expanded self-reflexive consciousness emerges to organize their inner functioning and ability to adapt. In the department, this consciousness circulates best through open, honest communication. Feedback is literally the self-correcting intelligence of the organism, the way the totality informs its individual parts of the need to adapt. By drawing on the reservoir of knowledge, creativity, and experience of all members, it supports greater individual and organizational consciousness and performance.

I was struck by the parallel between the inner work Mark was doing on himself and the scientific work of his department. A key mission of their research was to support the development of the purest possible materials for the optical fiber used in wiring the planet for the Internet.

The company manufactures telecommunications products for the most efficient transmission of information on pulses of light through ultra-high-purity glass fibers. They are, in effect, developing a medium that can transmit consciousness via light around the globe. Mark was enacting within himself the same transformative process in microcosm. As he worked on himself, he was also engaged in becoming the purest possible material for transmitting consciousness. By inviting and receiving the feedback of the department, he purified the fiber of courage and transformed their information into the light of self-knowledge.

A Year Later

Throughout the next year, Mark honored his commitments to work on himself and improve his relationships with the department as a whole and with each member individually. While we saw genuine improvement in these areas, and a reduction in interpersonal conflict and cynicism among department members, the integration of the department and its strategic direction was less successful. The two-day team-building retreat increased understanding between the three functionally separate groups, although no amount of talking could effectively integrate their real-time division of labor and diverse interests. Mark attempted to give his department greater voice in their strategic direction. A strategy planning group, formed at the retreat, met a number of times and began to develop a preliminary strategy. But it didn't provide the coherent direction the department required. In the meantime, the company hired an expert in the scientific specialization of the department to replace Mark as manager and to give greater strategic direction to the group.

Mark accepted a new assignment in a strategic operation that the company is counting on to compete successfully in the rapidly expanding market for global telecommunications products. The self-awareness, personal growth, and interpersonal skills Mark had developed over the past year have already served him well in his new position, and will continue to do so in whatever leadership roles he may hold in the future.

Jobs come and go. Departments rise and fall. Strategies change constantly. Businesses succeed and fail. Whatever the outcome, the ultimate beneficiary was Mark. As Mark reviewed the feedback experience a year later, he made the following reflections.

• I'm more comfortable and trusting of the individuals who went through the feedback with me.

• I'm more comfortable with the department as a whole (more openness and respect in group meetings, all of us "playing our positions" better.)

• I'm far more willing to let people take responsibility.

• I feel properly prepared for my new role.

• The department can run on its own better, though there is still much left undone: strategy, technical communications, etc.

• One of the most powerful things was my role as a coach. I couldn't play the game for them, but that role/self-vision gave me the power to give them feedback, overcoming my difficulties with assertiveness.

• What's helped in my current job is realizing there is a whole new group of people counting on me for leadership.

• The "wave on the ocean" self-view has eliminated many ego-based frustrations associated with recognition, position, career movement, etc. The success of the department is the greatest recognition I can receive. Yet being a wave—broad based, smooth, powerfully uplifting with an exuberant top—is a self-view that can keep me going in any role.

• [This experience] may serve to remind me that things may be even worse than they appear, but that I have the tools to deal with them.

This entire process was an extraordinary experience of courage. It takes courage to be open, to examine yourself honestly, to request and listen attentively to feedback from peers and subordinates, to face the truth, to communicate your learning candidly with others, and to act on this input and insight to change constructively. This is the stand the company is requiring of its leadership in its quest for high-performance. No one really understands what that requires until he or she submits to being tempered in the fire. By giving himself fully to this process, Mark demonstrated—in the best tradition of leading by example—the qualities of authentic leadership.

VI

TOOLS OF MASTERY

Practice is enlightenment.
—*Zen Master Dogen*

The Paradox of Practice

The qualities of mastery and awakened leadership needed to meet the current challenges remain nice-sounding abstractions until we put them into practice. This chapter describes key tools I have provided to support people in directing their creative energy toward individual development and high performance. They derive from a body of practices used in the world wisdom traditions for millennia to release and develop our potential, generate mastery and effectiveness in living, and reveal the inherent peace and well-being of our true nature.

Practice is where the rubber hits the road. Rigorous application of techniques produces real results in our consciousness, feelings, and behavior. In the long run it is committed practice that distinguishes the accomplished adept from the intellectual discussing high-sounding concepts. The techniques I draw from have been tested and refined over thousands of years of experimentation. They work if we use them appropriately. The adaptations I have made for the contemporary mentality and situation are minor at best, and follow the pattern of the centuries in which different cultures adapt the fundamental tools to fit their unique context.

These tools are relevant to both aspects of the process of self-realization—self-actualization and self-transcendence. Some techniques are "self-actualizing": They support the individual to cultivate characteristics, skills, experience, and behaviors that bring us to mastery and the fullness of what we could be. Self-actualization takes place within the dualistic framework of belief in a separate individual seeking fulfillment. It is grounded in the identification with the individual "I" and aims to create a stable, effective ego in the world. This process may continue until the pull of self-transcendence leads us to see through the individual "I" and realize our deeper identity with the underlying being-consciousness-energy. Ironically, in realizing the transcendent Self, our individual potential is freed up to make our full contribution to life.

I often refer to the paradox of practice. Practice is simultaneously a means and an end, a way to develop and attain, as well as an expression of our already-always true nature that needs no development or attainment. "Practice," from the Greek *praktos,* means to pass through or over, to experience or transact. That is, by passing through it you experience its benefits, and in so doing, you transcend it. Practice, then, is the disciplined process of effort that generates effortlessness.

At first, practice seems like an exercise you work at. It may feel awkward and uncomfortable, like beginning to practice a musical instrument. When I first started learning the guitar, my fingers ached, they didn't reach, my hands cramped. Yet through consistent application, at a certain point, the effort gave way to effortlessness and the music started to flow. I remember watching with amazement as my fingers moved smoothly, gracefully along the fretboard. It seemed that the music was playing itself and my fingers intuitively knew what to do. They could improvise, and played chords and notes I had never combined in that way before. Pure creativity showed up through the mastery of the form. Freedom had come through the discipline of practice.

At this stage, "practice" is no longer striving to attain or accomplish. It becomes more akin to the idea of the practice of medicine. In this sense, it is the masterful expression and demonstration of skill and accomplishment. And while learning is ongoing, the continuous improvement occurs within the context of mastery.

The most critical requirement for successful practice is to be fully committed to it. This means you are earnestly dedicated to regular, consistent practice, whether or not you feel like it that day. It also calls for gentle patience with ourselves, in which we let the process unfold in its own time, accepting the pace and each moment's experience. Some days it is easier, other days harder; some days there are clear results, other days not. We learn to allow the experience to be what it is, without judgment, and continually reapply ourselves to the practice.

In Zen it is said, "Practice is enlightenment." In the non-dual approach, when we sit to meditate we are not seeking to attain enlightenment, but to express it. To sit is to recognize the perfection of our true nature, to see that we do not have to attain what is already so, but merely to be it. In the Indian Advaita tradition this is often called the pathless path, that which brings you to where you already are. The ultimate punch line is best captured in Gahan Wilson's classic cartoon of the two Zen monks sitting in meditation, one with a look of dismay or puzzlement on his face as the other says: "Nothing happens next. This is it."

Meditation: The Practice of Being Conscious

Meditation, the practice of being conscious, enhances your awareness of simply being. In a workaholic culture addicted to endless doing—to the ongoing productivity of more, better, and different—it is suspect and threatening to simply *be*. It is a tremendous challenge to an accomplishment-oriented mentality to understand this basic principle: the key to productivity is knowing how to be unproductive.

This doesn't mean merely getting rest in order to replenish your energy. When you truly see that being comes first, that it is the powerful source of all doing, then you will value and take refuge in your own being. Letting yourself be and becoming conscious of what you truly are, are one and the same process. All our doing will never attain the peace, fulfillment, and well-being that is already within us. As Paul Valery wrote, "The best way to make your dreams come true is to wake up."

To be conscious is to be aware. It is to be present with what is, as it is, to see clearly into the nature of things. It is based on paying attention, focusing your awareness. Vietnamese Zen master Thich Nhat Hanh, nominated by Martin Luther King for the Nobel Peace Prize, calls this the most basic precept of all: simply to be aware of what we do, what we are, each minute.

In contemporary western Buddhism, the practice of moment-to-moment awareness is called mindfulness. It derives from the ancient Theravadin Buddhist practice known as *vipassana,* which literally means "insight" or a clear seeing into the reality of things. It's another word for being here now, fully present and attentive. Mindfulness is applied to a wide spectrum of experience. In a progressive sequence of techniques the practitioner becomes mindful of breath, thought, sensation, speech, movement, action, other people, and environment. Most of the specific exercises that follow are variants of the basic practice of mindfulness meditation, starting with the ground technique of breath awareness.

Breath Awareness Meditation

Attention on the breath is a widely used and effective method for cultivating the inner awareness at the source of relaxation and peace of mind. The process of following the breath can dissolve stressful mental, emotional, and physical states and create a calming effect for harmony and inner balance.

You may sit cross-legged on the floor, or comfortably relaxed in a chair, with your head, neck, and back straight. It helps to hold your head as if a string is attached from the crown of the head to a balloon which is floating above you and gently lifting the top of your head. If sitting in a chair, it is best to keep arms and legs uncrossed.

Let the belly be soft and the shoulders relaxed. I recommend closing your eyes as well, to encourage undistracted inner focus. If you prefer to keep them open, then fix your attention on a spot on the floor three to four feet ahead of you.

Simply pay attention to the breath. It is best to breathe through the nostrils, not the mouth. It's not necessary to take deep breaths or to regulate the breath. Just notice your breathing without any attempt at control. Be gentle, don't push or force.

Observe the in-and-out of the breath through the nostrils. Note the coolness of the in-breath at the tip of the nose. Listen to the sound of the breathing. It will quiet down as relaxation proceeds. Note the rising and falling of the lungs and diaphragm. Then select one area of concentration—the tip of the nose, the sound of the breath, or the lungs, for example—and keep your attention there for the whole exercise.

Let thoughts and feelings come and go freely, but keep bringing your attention back to your breathing. You will notice the tendency to attach to thinking and to dwell on thoughts. Most people are either fascinated by thoughts and indulge them, or repulsed and try to stop them or push them away. For this exercise, however, simply sit and observe, allowing thoughts to rise and disappear without judging or trying to control them, neither pushing or pulling at them.

Do nothing about your thoughts except notice them and then bring your attention back to the breath. Typically, as you sit following the breath, a thought will come along and you will be drawn to focus on it. As soon as you notice that you're thinking, no matter what the thought, return attention to the breath. Let the breath become a quiet, peaceful focus that you return to over and over again. This process will relax and revitalize you.

As you learn to bring attention back to the breath, you'll notice gaps between the thoughts, quiet spaces in which there is just silence, emptiness, peace. Simply be aware of the quietness and abide there until another thought arises. Then return attention to the breath and remain with the breath until you note the silence again.

It's important not to judge your meditation experience. Some times are quiet, some are busy with noisy and active thoughts. Whatever the experience, simply observe and return to the breathing. There is no right or wrong meditation experience, merely what is showing up in the moment. Cultivating non-expectation and self-acceptance allows it all to come and go freely. Just as patience, perseverance, and a sense of humor bear the fruits of equanimity, so do wisdom and freedom become available to us through dedicated practice

It's best to begin by devoting at least twenty minutes for this exercise. An optimal program would involve a regular, daily practice of thirty to sixty minutes in the morning and another session of equal length in the late afternoon or evening. This practice can also be used at any time of the day when you are stressed. Just sit down and follow the procedure—even five minutes at your desk produces relief. Eventually, you'll be able to apply this technique throughout the course of everyday living and working, while walking, driving (eyes open!) and, as you progress, even during your interactions with people.

Regular practice of this simple technique produces a sense of peace, well-being, and greater vitality. It develops mental clarity for creative thinking and better decision-making. It cultivates a sharpened attention to detail and the ability to listen with greater receptivity to others. By providing a center to dwell in, it reduces our reactivity to life and enables us to respond more appropriately to people and our experience.

The technique enhances emotional balance and personal health. It is used often in pain management and healing. It reduces the risks of stress-based diseases and has positive effects on many neurophysiological and biochemical processes.

Ultimately, this practice serves as a primary doorway to self-knowledge. It opens practitioners to intuition and inner guidance, providing access to deeper realms of consciousness and spiritual development. It enables you to see things as they really are, to know reality without conditioning or preconceptions. It is the basic ground for full awakening and human freedom.

Mindfulness of Mind

It's amazing what you can observe just by watching. —Yogi Berra

The next step in mindfulness is to pay full attention to the flow of thoughts, judgments, attitudes, desires, fears, memories, hopes, and dreams that make up what we call "mind." This practice enables us to cut through what the Tibetan master Chögyam Trungpa Rinpoche ironically dubbed "the epitome of the human realm . . . to be stuck in a huge traffic jam of discursive thought." It allows us to develop a penetrating clarity into the specific content of thought that generates our experience. It provides a close up view of the mechanism that both defines the individual self and sustains our suffering.

To practice mindfulness effectively requires an abiding interest in how life works and a strong desire to know yourself. You need a consistent inner drive to focus and refocus your attention on what's really happening with you. It calls for you to be uncompromisingly honest with yourself, willing to face and recognize your experience and the basic patterns that drive you. When we commit to this unflinching observation, we finally see how subtle and deep are the layers of self-deception.

The practice starts from the ground technique of breath awareness. In the original breath awareness exercise, you took no note of the thought except to realize that your attention had wandered, and then you refocused on the breath. In this practice, the goal is to get greater insight into the nature of the thought itself. Here, you take note of the thought, perhaps briefly labeling it—for example, "hoping," "anticipating," or "remembering" —then let it go and refocus attention on the breath. Then recognize the next thought that comes up, and again let go and refocus on your breathing. This practice is the simple process of noticing, letting go, and refocusing on breath again and again.

You gradually become familiar with the way your mind works. You see its typical, habitual patterns, desires, and fears. You see how fascinated and attached you are to certain patterns, and how that attachment holds them in place, feeds them, and generates your experience and perception of life. Becoming conscious in this way allows you to deal with and, ultimately, be free of unconscious patterns of thought. You are less likely to get sucked into the compulsive chatter of mind. As you become more able to note and let go of habitual tendencies, you become more centered, less reactive, and more genuinely responsive to what life brings. Some patterns may disappear gradually, others may stop arising altogether.

Eventually the practice develops a penetrating clarity, enabling you to pay more attention to detail, do better quality work, and make fewer mistakes. Your ability to be consciously present in the moment grows stronger. As your sense of who you are shifts from being the experiencer to being the watcher of your experience, greater depths of self-knowledge and freedom are revealed.

Identifying Limitations and Obstacles

In the workplace, I have adapted mindfulness to support people in identifying the specific limiting beliefs and operating principles that create obstacles to their self-development and the accomplishment of their goals. It enables them to discern the effects of the underlying assumptions of incompletion and separation, and the survival strategies of desire and fear discussed in chapter four. These effects show up in individual consciousness and behavior, as well as in the basic norms and processes that govern organizational morale, motivation, and performance.

I support individuals and teams to become clear about their limiting operating principles, determine what holds them in place, and identify the effects—both wanted and unwanted—that these patterns produce in their experience. When people can clearly identify the effects these beliefs have on their work and life, they finally have some basis for making a choice about whether they will continue to hold on to, or let go of, those patterns.

Limiting operating principles are strongly held beliefs usually derived from decisions we made in early life based on insufficient evidence. They determine the limits of our experience. They define what is possible for us, create a comfort zone of familiar experience, and provide us with a self-image that we're reluctant to change or leave even when it restricts us.

Because this structure of interpretation forms a filter that limits or distorts our perceptions, we tend to perceive selectively, seeing mostly what matches our conditioning and beliefs. In addition, the mind takes the further step of using the data we perceive to reinforce its original beliefs, thus creating a self-fulfilling cycle of self-justification. These beliefs become strongly held habits that go so deep into us that they have neurophysiological effects in our bodies.

Since the inborn ability and potential within us are shaped by these underlying beliefs, neither talent, desire, nor willpower is sufficient to produce deep or lasting change unless we also resolve the limiting operating principles at work unconsciously.

The first step to resolving these limiting principles is to become fully aware of them. We begin by identifying the operating principles that restrict your effectiveness in work or leadership. Some examples may be helpful. Let's look first at typical beliefs about oneself, which comprise the standard limiting self-talk that undermines self-confidence. They are all basic variations on the theme of being flawed or incomplete.

I'm not okay, I'm imperfect, flawed, incomplete, not whole.
I'm unworthy, undeserving, weak, inadequate, incompetent,
   unlovable.
I can't do it, can't handle it, will screw it up, always do it wrong.
I'm the victim of life, powerless, out of control, unable to shape my
   life.

Once we develop some self-doubt, our inherent survival tendency is
to seek ways out of it, to make ourselves all right. Ironically, many of
these approaches just lead us deeper into the quicksand of limitation.
For example, one unworkable strategy, grounded in the belief in separation and the yearning to overcome it, just gets us stuck in dependency on other people:

I'm okay if other people think I'm okay.
My worth or well-being is dependent on others.
I must have love, acceptance, approval. I must avoid rejection,
   disapproval.
I must be nice, do the right thing, say yes to everyone's requests.

These may even escalate to the level of co-dependency where our
well-being is pegged to being there for others, another ineffective vari-
ant on the quest to transcend separation and justify oneself:

I'm okay if I'm helping others or being useful.
I must be all things to all people.
I'm responsible for other people's well-being, feelings, lives,
   problems.
I need people to need me.
I'm guilty, anxious, or upset when others have problems that are
   beyond me.
I must be in control of others.
I'm bored or worthless without a problem to solve or someone to
   help.

Another typical pattern—dependency on work and accomplishment for our sense of well-being—has traditionally been more present in male conditioning. But as more women enter the work force, it may be increasingly relevant to them as well. These beliefs, of course, are the underlying bases for workaholism, and are especially stinging in times of layoffs and high unemployment:

I'm okay as long as I'm working, being productive, accomplishing.
My well-being depends on what I do, how much I accomplish, how hard I work.
I must do more, better, different.
There is never enough time.
I shouldn't take breaks and vacations. Relaxation is unproductive.

Then there are the assaults of compulsive perfectionism:

I can make myself perfect by doing everything perfectly all the time.
I must not make mistakes. Mistakes invalidate me, they are failures.
I can't do things perfectly because I'm not perfect and never will be.
I must look good, be professional, not show doubt, confusion, or weakness.
I must be the expert. People expect me to know it all.
Life should not have problems.
Everything should work out smoothly, the way I want.
If things don't work out well, there must be something wrong with me.

Beliefs that drive individual self-sufficiency become limitations when they block our effectiveness for leadership or teamwork and collaboration.

If you want it done right—or quicker—do it yourself.
Be self-reliant, don't trust your fate to someone else.
I've got to win, be first, look good, stand out, be right.
You can't trust people, they will rip you off, let you down.

Having identified your limiting beliefs, the next step is to take responsibility for them by noting the payoffs you get for holding onto them. That is, we usually hold on to our assumptions because we unconsciously believe they will serve our survival in some way, either by getting us something we desire or by helping us avoid something we fear. It is our attachment to these desires and fears that usually lock us into the pattern.

Typical payoffs might include our quest for power and control, our need to win or to avoid loss. Or, we yearn for love, seek approval and recognition, and consequently fear disapproval, rejection, and criticism. Some of us are on a perpetual treadmill seeking to prove ourselves, justifying, documenting, being right, innocent, attempting to demonstrate how righteous or superior we are.

Or we might be pursuing intensity, excitement, drama, and risk, and thus avoiding boredom and routine. On the other hand, many of us cling to comfort and security, ease, and safety, avoiding pain, effort, risk, or conflict and confrontation. We may seek the familiar and fear the unknown, prefer order over creativity and peace over risk, even though the risky way might promise great success. Indeed, those attached to success and accomplishment are likely to fear failure or falling short. If work is the avenue to fame, fortune, and status, then we may relentlessly seek the limelight, raises, and promotions without due consideration of the costs to us and others around us.

We are freed from these limiting patterns when we release our grip on the desires and fears that hold them in place. We can let go of these deeply entrenched survival strategies when we come more closely in touch with our true nature. When we recognize the power of the Self already within us, we can give up the quest for power. We can be freed of the yearning to be loved when we dwell in our own self-acceptance and value our whole being. We find lasting safety and security in our surrender to destiny and our eternal, transcendental nature. We experience intensity and enthusiasm in the joy of knowing our freedom. When we know our own Self, the need for self-justification disappears

Once you've identified your own particular network of self-limiting thoughts, you're in a position to make some choices. Which ones are you willing to assume responsibility for? Which ones are you ready to let go of? Which ones are you willing to accept and let be as they are?

Recognizing that some grooves are too deep, or not worth meddling with, may lead you to the liberating wisdom of self-acceptance. And finally, which patterns are you willing to change?

I do not assume that people "should" change their beliefs. This assumption has been the source of violence, oppression, and dogmatism throughout history. I've learned that working with people's beliefs is a subtle and powerful process that is also a minefield of possibly explosive reactions. We need to approach it with sensitivity, respect for others' values and experience, and the humility that we don't have the answer for everyone. This is especially so for people committed to discussing "spirituality" or "wisdom" in the workplace who may forget that everything we have to say—anything that can be conceptualized at all—is another relative belief that cannot grasp or convey the elusive, unspeakable Truth.

In my work I prefer that people investigate the impact of their beliefs on themselves and their colleagues, their work and organizations, and then freely decide for themselves what is appropriate. Empowerment here arises from their own awareness, their willingness to make choices consistent with their deepest values, and their commitment to be responsible for their choices and live with integrity.

If people do choose to change, there is a simple technology for transforming limiting operating principles into more positive and expansive beliefs. It is amazing how a small shift in thinking can produce powerful changes in feeling and behavior when people finally see the mechanism and how to work with it.

The Technology of Creation

Once we understand how mind creates experience, we are able to use the powerful techniques of the wisdom traditions to shape our experience in directions we choose. These tools work from the inside to bring forth desired qualities, characteristics, abilities, and skills from the formless sea of potentiality within us. The process of self-creation is an activity of the dualistic mode of consciousness which divides itself into subject and object and then lives as a creative individual seeking to self-actualize. While we operate here within the egoic point of view, we are actually replicating in microcosm the cosmic process of creation itself.

Thought creates. Thought or imagination is the instrument by which the formless source-consciousness manifests creation. This is happening now whether we know it or not, in the same way that the law of gravity works whether we recognize or not. When we live in alignment with gravity, we can be more effective in its domain. When we are conscious of how mind works, it becomes our instrument not our master.

The process of self-creation, as the mature expression of a functional, creative ego-mind, starts when you take full responsibility for creating your experience and taking charge of your life. Responsibility involves a shift in your sense of self from dependent victim to proactive cause. From the Latin root *re-spondere*, to promise, it means being accountable or able to answer for one's conduct; answerable as the primary cause, motive, or agent; having the character of a free moral agent.

Being responsible means that you cease to view yourself as a passive leaf blown around at the effect of powerful forces beyond your control. You live as agent, creating your life, rather than it "happening to you." You acknowledge your autonomy, your sense of personal independence, and act as if your survival and destiny are in your own hands. You live proactively, shaping your life direction. You are self-motivated, you do what needs to be done without having to be told. You live from choice, not "have to." Living from "have to" creates a sense of obligation, duty, and burden that leads to resentment, blame, complaining, low energy, low morale, and poor performance. Living from choice energizes and motivates.

You recognize that you create your feelings, reactions, actions, and behaviors. This lets you see that you are the source of your happiness or unhappiness, your satisfaction or dissatisfaction. You accept accountability for your experience and do not blame others. No one *makes* you think, feel, or do anything. This ownership releases your power that had been locked up in upset emotions and reactions. When you see that you are causing your experience, you are free to redirect that power in ways you choose.

We direct our energy through the focusing of intention and attention. As the traditional wisdom says, what you focus on you create. Intentionality, the purposeful, ongoing commitment to a desired outcome, is the driving force behind creation. Intention literally takes the creative power of desire—the survival drive of the egoic mind—to its fullest expression by channeling all of our desire in a single direction. Attention is a focusing of awareness. If we think of consciousness as light, and awareness as diffused light, then attention has the extraordinary concentrated power of a laser. Attention and intention together work like a laser that sends neurotransmitters coursing through the neural network of our organism, much like the lasers that send pulses of light-information through the optical fiber of the global nervous system. The mysterious drama of creation flows through our organism.

We must be careful how we focus the power of consciousness. We are working literally with the awesome energy of life itself, a power so hot it can burn or fry you. Here is the divine power of the Self that can create or destroy. The world wisdom traditions caution us to approach this power with respect and humility, and to use it only for noble ends that do no harm to others. Like the nuclear energy which can give off toxic radioactivity, so this internal power has its own corrosive effects on consciousness and experience. The abuse of power is an ever-present danger and temptation for the egoic mentality. My intent here is strictly on developing seeds of potential within your own bodymind organism that serve your self-actualization and your harmony with others.

Two fundamental tools that I have been using in my work for twenty years together provide a whole-brained approach to self-development: the left-brain activity of declaration and the right-brain modality of visualization.

Declaration

The greatest discovery of my generation is that human beings, by changing the inner attitudes of their minds, can change the outer aspects of their lives. —William James

Mind is a two-edged sword. Just as certain beliefs and operating principles can limit our experience, so can empowering beliefs expand our experience and strengthen our behavior in ways we choose to develop. The most effective tool for transforming our beliefs is the practice of declaration, popularly referred to as positive self-talk or affirmation.

We can grasp the creative power of declaration by contrasting it with another form of speech called an assertion. An assertion describes what is: "My car is in the parking lot." The assertion is either right or wrong, true or false, and we can prove or document it by getting evidence or using logic. We can go out there and see the car.

Declarations, on the other hand, do not describe experience, they create it. At work, managers make all kinds of declarations that create new circumstances for people: "You're hired," "You're fired," "You're promoted." Strategic visions and mission statements of what we stand for or where we are going are declarations. Statements of values are declarations.

Declarations have the power to change what is in the act of speaking about it. If two people want to get married, they go to a justice of the peace or priest who declares them husband and wife. A change occurred in the speaking, just as Congress can declare a war into existence, or a baseball umpire declares balls and strikes. Its not where the ball actually is—not an assertion—it's what the ump says it is. A famous ump responded to the inquisitive batter wanting to know if the pitch was a ball or a strike: "It ain't nothing till I call it."

Declarations are not right or wrong, they are either valid or invalid. The validity of the declaration depends on the authority of the speaker. The ump has the authority and if you disagree with him, he throws you out of the game. Only those invested with the proper authority can legally marry you. Only those managers with the proper authority can hire and fire. The issue for your own declarations, of course, is if you acknowledge your own authority to make the declaration. And how do you get that authority? You take it.

As a former historian, I like to remind people that declaration is the ultimate patriotic act. The United States of America was literally created by the Declaration of Independence. Note they didn't call it the "Assertion of Independence." Based on the evidence, we were a colony of the King of England. Yet, in 1776, some of our forefathers informed King George III and the world at large that they were no longer a colony of Great Britain, but a free and sovereign nation. They brilliantly declared "certain truths to be self-evident"—no need for proof here—and appealed to the Creator who has given us "inalienable rights"—hard to argue with that. They literally declared their freedom and, equally brilliantly, declared a new basis of authority—popular sovereignty—that government derives its just authority from the consent of the governed. While they pulled the rug out from under the old divine right of kings, they wisely appealed to the "Supreme Judge of the world for the rectitude of our intentions." Basically, they, and we as their heirs, were free because they said so.

Of course, they had to fight the War of Independence. The key question here is: When were they free? When they signed the Declaration in 1776, or after they drove the British out? It is clear to me that they were free the moment they signed the document. Only free people, not colonists, fought the War of Independence, just as only free people engaged in the many slave revolts in our history. Slaves do not revolt. They were "free" the moment they said so, regardless of conditions. Freedom is a declaration, not an assertion, and there are free people in prison or poverty just as there are affluent slaves in corporate America.

What made them free was not only their declaration, but their willingness to stake everything on its truth: "And, for the support of this declaration, with a firm reliance on the protection of Divine Providence, we mutually pledge to each other our lives, our fortunes, and our sacred honour." When you are willing to take that kind of stand in your truth, it shows up for you. In the long run, nothing less will do.

When we design affirmations and practice self-talk, we are living out the mysterious process of becoming what we already are. As Ramana Maharshi told us, "The state of self-realization is not attaining something new or reaching some goal that is far away, but simply being that which you always are and which you always have been, simply being yourself." The "realizing" he speaks of has two aspects. One is to recognize what is already so. The other is to make real, to bring from the potential to the actual, and to experience fully—not just as a concept—what is true in our depths. A declaration brings forth seed potentialities of our inherent nature, waters them and nurtures them to maturity. It brings life-giving vitality to the genetic coding within the acorn and allows the tree of actualization to flower.

The simple process of self-talk is to affirm what is possible for you and to identify with the intended outcome as a present reality. You declare to yourself that you have already accomplished your goal or become what you want to be. The declaration is internally spoken by yourself to yourself. I have found it usually works best to keep this internal and private, not spoken out loud or to others. Through conscious internal repetition, the affirmation has the power to become self-fulfilling by changing your fundamental beliefs about yourself or life.

Repetition creates belief. It is not a very sophisticated method. Thoughts we sustain long enough and with enough intensity seem real to us. It was unconscious repetition that gave our limiting beliefs so much power to begin with, and the same process applies to the declaration as well. Repetition is the basic key to learning: Remember how we learned to write, or to ride a bike, or develop technical skills. In fact learning and brainwashing are both based on the power of repetition to change consciousness. The main distinction is that "we" educate, "they" brainwash. Positive self-talk is a way we wash our own brain and scrub it of the accretions of the past so the new can shine. Belief, in turn, shapes our experience, feelings, and behaviors. Once the declaration becomes part of our operating system, behavior and experience flow naturally and spontaneously from it.

There are four key elements to designing and using affirmations. First, only affirm what you truly believe is possible, that is, what you believe you are capable of and what the laws of life will allow. This is actually quite open-ended, since the history of humanity and high performance is a systematic record of people regularly doing the impossible—that is, shattering what others and even science claimed was impossible. Formulate your vision of that possibility by using personal pronouns and focus on the positive qualities you wish to develop. Watch out for emphasizing what you don't want. Since the tendency of mind is to create what you focus on, if you affirm "I am not angry," the power of attention is still on the anger. One of the basic drawbacks to self-creation is that people often focus on what they don't want, not on what they do, and then wonder why it so difficult to experience it. Finally, frame your affirmation in the present tense. If you keep affirming "I will be happy," you simply create a belief that remains in the future. Of course, the future never happens. When the belief is created in the present tense, once the belief kicks in, it happens now, which is the only time there is.

Here are some sample affirmations:

I am okay. My well-being and worth come from within me.
I believe in my ability to handle what life gives me.
I am relaxed and confident in tense or emotional situations.
I welcome change and the surprises of life.
I enjoy the challenge of living at risk.
I accept mistakes and errors as opportunities for growth and learning.
I love the radiant, healthy feeling I get with my lean, firm body.
I am filled with vitality and enthusiasm for living.
I see the humor in life and share it lightly with people.
I give myself permission to relax and nourish myself.
My creativity flows spontaneously.
I trust intuition and inner guidance.

Here is another set, specifically designed for leaders and workplace experience:

My role is to serve and support people to succeed.
I walk my talk and model the behaviors I seek in others.
I consciously work to solve problems and meet challenges.
I have a passion for customers and make their issues a priority.
I act decisively in the face of ambiguity.
I convey a sense of confidence and optimism.
I communicate performance expectations clearly.
I hold people accountable for achieving results.
I have a clear sense of who we are, what we stand for, and where we are going.
I connect all our activities and processes to the big picture.
I keep focused on the important activities in the midst of crises.
I am aware of the unseen potential in others and support them to realize it.

I encourage and reward risk-taking.

I celebrate others' success and provide rewards and recognition of their efforts.

I give constructive feedback to foster individual growth.

I seek to understand the views of others from their perspective.

I encourage others to express divergent views.

I work to find creative solutions that benefit all.

I value and seek out others' insights and listen well to their input.

I am open to receiving constructive feedback and critical review of my work.

I am willing to change my views and actions in the light of new information.

I care for my well-being and encourage others to do the same.

I take time to find meaning and enjoyment in life.

I value and create an environment that supports the rich diversity of views, approaches, talents, and perspectives of all the people.

I actively mentor and coach individuals.

Self talk is really a conversation with yourself. You tell yourself who or what you are. You speak your truth to yourself. And, simultaneously, you listen, you pay attention to yourself. To truly speak and listen to yourself is the ultimate monologue, the self-talk of the Self as its generates its own form.

Declaration is the rational principle, the logos, the assertive procreative thrust that gives shape to the formless dynamic potentiality. This verbal, linear process literally de-fines (puts an "end" on) the form of the new, literally creates boundaries around it and gives it outline. This is the way the formless source takes form and generates its endless becoming through mental activity.

Visualization

If you can see it, you can become it. —Walt Disney

The two-dimensional, left-brain approach of declaration is given a fuller dimensionality through the imaging activity of right-brain consciousness. Here we employ visualization, and the other senses if appropriate, to deepen and extend our ability to create experience.

Visualization is the active practice of consciously focusing on mental pictures and sense impressions to create intended results and experiences. It gives rigor to a simple mental faculty most of us experience daily: daydreaming, fantasizing, anticipating, dreaming, remembering. For whatever purpose, we all have entertained pictures in mind.

Many sacred traditions practice some form of visualization. Devout Christians have meditated on the qualities of the saints and the passion of Jesus in order to take on those characteristics. Buddhist and Hindu tantric practitioners follow highly detailed, precise methods for visualizing both the abstract forms of the *yantras* (symbolic diagrams) and the anthropomorphic characteristics of deities who represent certain qualities. Secular visualization practice—used, for example, in mind-body healing and personal growth—likewise lays out a systematic method of use.

Visualization works according to basic principles of consciousness. It is said that imagery is a principal language of the unconscious. When the unconscious communicates with the conscious mind, it often does so through dreams or visions. Therefore, if we want to communicate with the deepest realm of consciousness, it makes sense to send it a picture. When we hold an image of ourselves living out the declaration fully, in the depths of mind we think that is really happening.

To the unconscious, "seeing is believing." The nervous system doesn't distinguish between a well-imagined picture and physical reality. Mental images trigger neurophysiological experiences similar to those caused by perceptions of physical events. As a child, I had recurring dreams of being chased by a monster. I would be running, frightened, getting all hot and sweaty. When I woke up in bed, I was relieved, of course, to know it was only a dream. Yet I was hot, sweaty, and tired. How did I get these real physical experiences if it was only "imagination"?

We are learning from psychoneuroimmunology that strongly held images produce identifiable neurophysiological and biochemical effects in the body. In my dream I thought I was running, and the unconscious sent messages to the sweat glands to sweat. And so they did. Mind sent messages to the muscles that they were running. And so they were tired. Imagination generates experience. The physical is a response to the image, a crystallization and condensing of the subtle light of consciousness.

The movie of mind is lived out in the drama of the mindbody organism. It is like going to the cinema. When you sit down in the theater and the film starts, you know it's just a movie, just light projecting moving pictures, forms, colors on the screen. Yet if the movie is a good one we get drawn into the drama and co-experience it vicariously with the actors. When they are happy, we are happy, when they are sad, we are sad, when they are sexually aroused, so are we. In the same way, we are sucked into the drama of imagination and flesh it out in our experience. So when we visualize ourselves happy or fulfilled or courageous, we are sending neural signals to the mindbody organism that this is happening and to experience it. In this way, the mind projects and receives the world simultaneously. It projects the movie on the screen of consciousness, and through that consciousness creates the full-bodied experience.

Visualization, sometimes called psychomotor rehearsal training, is a common part of high-performance athletic training. It is used for perfecting the golf swing or baseball stance, refining diving and gymnastic form, even for teamwork with basketball teams and other similar uses. At one point both U.S. and Soviet Olympic athletes were using these mental techniques in up to 75% of their training time. It is also widely practiced by actors, public speakers, trial lawyers, and other aspiring performance artists.

Moreover, imagined events that are imprinted deeply in the mind are also recorded by the brain and central nervous system as memories. That is, just as the mind stores records of real events in memory, it also stores records of imagined events in the same library. Hence it is often—and progressively so as we age!—difficult to distinguish between what "really" happened and what we imagine happened. This may be a problem in some areas of our lives, but it helps the visualization process. If you picture yourself as patient, the mind stores it in the same memory bank as real events. Say you do that three times a day for six months. You now have a long record of events of being patient. The accumulation of these memories becomes the basis for creating a new self-image of being a patient person. And from self-image flows experience.

Vision has always been a primary way we motivate and uplift ourselves toward great accomplishment and new behavior. Like Moses, great leaders throughout history have tenaciously held a positive vision of the Promised Land to guide and inspire their people. Current leaders have developed a contemporary, if not always so uplifting, version in the organizational visions which have the same intention of focusing people on desired end results to shape their experience.

The same principle of motivation is exploited in contemporary advertising, the current master of the high-powered image. TV commercials, magazines, and billboards all want to lure you into the picture. If you can see yourself in or with their product, the sale is virtually made. It is the strategy behind encouraging you to try on the new dress or coat in the clothing store, or test drive the new car you are "just looking" at. Once you see yourself in it, you begin to develop a new self-image of yourself in the car or the coat. When you go back to your old one, you measure it unconsciously according to the new standard and it just isn't as good any more. All the dents and rust on the old car, the worn quality of the old coat, show up. The vision of the new is a more attractive standard that pulls you toward it. In the movies, they show you the trailers to interest you in the coming film. Each time you visualize yourself in a new way, it is like a coming attraction to the full-length feature which is on its way. The part of you that wants that movie to be real will come back for more. When there is total identification with the positive vision, then lasting change occurs within us.

There are simple guidelines for effective visualizations. Start by finding a comfortable space where you can relax and close your eyes. Then experiment with the breath awareness technique until the mind is quiet and receptive.

Basically, you are the director and actor in your own movie, so direct it the way you want and rehearse it as often as you like. Make it personal and see yourself ideally living out the qualities, experiences, and behaviors you are seeking to cultivate. Focus can be either internal or external. That is, you can see yourself as you usually do, from within your head looking out of your eyes; or you can see yourself from outside your body as an external observer might.

The more multi-sensory and three-dimensional the image, the better. So bring sound, taste, touch, and feelings into the picture as well.

Listen to your voice, feel your body sensations and emotions. Bring in as much vivid detail as you can. If it is difficult to get realistic pictures, metaphors and cartoons will do. In cancer therapy, Carl Simonton reported that a patient would imagine the seven dwarfs scooping up dead cancer cells from within them and carrying them out. Because pictures come and go rapidly, it's important to keep refocusing attention on the image you want. While you may not get clear, stable pictures, even the slightest glimpse of a new possibility is powerful. Indeed, in this practice less is more, and a minute or two of concentrated attention is worth more than ten minutes of idle day dreaming.

As you watch your own self-projected movie, you will again see how you are both cause and effect, agent and object, of the universal creative process. You are the imaginer, you are the imagined, and you are the imagining. From this perspective, you can witness the play of mind as the instrument of creation in which you are both the evolving individual and the changeless source.

The Body Scan: The Art of Feeling

The techniques we have discussed so far are mostly cerebral, with emphasis on thought and image. Now we direct our awareness deeper into the body to experience how consciousness *literally* plays us like an instrument that vibrates with the rich diversity of sensations, emotions, and energy flows we call feeling. It is through the physical that we directly experience the palpable reality of the fundamental energy that the Japanese call *ki* , the Chinese call *chi*, the Hindus call *shakti* or *prana*, also known in the West as the *élan vital*, the life force, the spirit. Whatever we call it, it is the dynamism within all experience, the life animating the organism. If we are open and feel it fully, we are brought home to the power of our own true Self.

The body scan derives from ancient techniques in both Hindu yoga and the vipassana practice of Buddhist India and Southeast Asia. It is as close as we can come to the art or science of feeling, which we discussed earlier as the basis for courage and compassion for others. This exercise in full feeling attention expands mindfulness to embrace emotional and physical sensations and bodily stress. It enables you to reduce or eliminate much of your tension, pain, and fatigue, and gives you more access to your inherent energy and vitality. More specifically, it allows you to process emotions and upsets wisely without having to dump them inappropriately on others or suffer the internal consequences of repression or suppression.

It is based on the understanding that stressful emotional and bodily states arise and develop into serious problems because 1) we don't notice them until they become extreme, and 2) we don't know how to handle them when we do notice them. The exercise enables you to monitor the flow of sensations in the body, detect emotional upset or stress as it is starting, and be able to experience it and let go of it before it builds into a problem.

As we pay attention to bodily feelings, we note that there is a continual movement of sensation—feelings of lightness and heaviness, hot and cold, tightness and looseness, tingling and numbness, pulsing and pounding, pleasure and pain. If we can accept them as they are and experience them fully, they come and go easily.

Ordinarily we tend to live mostly in our concepts and stories about these sensations rather than feeling them directly. This is akin to studying the map rather than traveling the territory, or eating the menu and not the meal. The intellect becomes a hiding place from the raw experience of life. Our attachment to concept and story—all those reasons *why* we feel as we do—is in fact an avoidance of feeling and, paradoxically, holds the sensations in place. When we are willing to let go of the whole mental drama of interpretation and be simply present to our experience, then we allow the movement of feeling to take its natural course.

Our reluctance or unwillingness to feel fully seems to be driven primarily by avoidance of pain. While we want to experience pleasure, we run from pain, which leads us to block and resist the flow of energy sensations. This not only cuts us off from the direct experience of pleasure and drives our ever-increasing demands for heightened experience. It also, paradoxically, increases our suffering as well. As the saying goes, what you resist, persists.

Often what we call pain or tension is a traffic jam or blockage of this flow of feeling—a contraction like the tightening of the fist. This very avoidance of unpleasantness locks the unpleasantness in place and allows it to build up into something worse. When we become sufficiently aware that we are contracting, we are able to let go in the same way that we can relax a fist.

The key is to notice the sensation, tension, or pain, feel it fully, and allow the contraction to relax. This involves courageously experiencing the discomfort of pain and tension. To take the pleasure and pain as they are also means that we allow them to go. If you have a headache, the willingness to be aware of and experience the pain will allow the headache to pass. Sensations are dynamic and moving, and it is only our holding on that keeps them in place. Feeling completes a sensation and frees it to disappear.

The body scan can be done either sitting cross-legged on the floor, sitting comfortably in a chair, or lying down on the back with the arms by the sides and the legs stretched out with the feet one or two feet apart.

Begin by following the breath for a few minutes. Then place your attention in the toes of the right foot and experience the sensations there. There may be tingling or numbness, or you may feel the pressure of your shoe. Just feel the sensations in the toes. If there is tension or pain, feel it completely and let it be. Keep full feeling attention in the toes of the right foot for about ten seconds.

Then move your attention to the bottom of the right foot and experience the sensations there. If you feel tension or pain, just experience it as it is and let it be. Keep your attention there for ten seconds, experiencing the sensations of the bottom of the foot.

The point is to follow the same procedure for all the parts of the body from the toes to the top of the head. A good order to follow is:

Right foot: toes, sole, instep, top, and ankle
Right leg: shin, calf, knee, upper leg, thigh, buttock
Left foot and leg: same order
Torso: genitals, pubic area, intestines, stomach, internal organs, diaphragm, abdomen, lungs, chest, breast, shoulders
Back: lower, middle, upper, shoulder blades, base of neck
Right arm, wrist, hand, knuckles, fingers, palm

Left arm: same order

Neck, chin, jaw, mouth, lips, tongue, cheeks, facial muscles

Eyes, eye sockets, eye lids, nose, forehead, temples, sides of face, head, ears

Skull and crown

Be sure to give a full ten seconds at least to each part of the body, experiencing the sensations present there.

Having reached the top of the head, simply allow your awareness to scan freely throughout the body, observing and feeling predominant sensations wherever they may arise. Keep attention on the physical sensations, without dwelling on thoughts. Whenever concepts occur, return your focus to the immediacy of the sensations.

Note that these feelings are continually arising, peaking, and dissolving throughout your body. Sensations rise and fall, ebb and flow, waves on the ocean of the basic life energy. If you simply remain open, allowing and feeling, this great reservoir will nourish and revitalize you.

After completing the body scan, return to following the breath and relax more deeply into the breathing. Remain in that state of deep relaxation until ready to come out. Reorient yourself by wiggling fingers and toes, moving the head from side to side, then swaying the torso, opening the eyes, and gradually moving the body until you feel grounded.

It's best to select a quiet, comfortable location where you won't be interrupted. Give yourself at least thirty minutes for the entire body scan, and add extra time for remaining in the deep relaxation at the end. If this done in a group, be sure to leave at least twenty minutes of grounding and discussion time after the exercise before ending the session. This exercise produces very deep states of relaxation, and people need sufficient reorientation time before returning to regular activities. For the same reason, it is specifically recommended at bedtime for insomnia and sleep disorders. Practicing this process at bedtime releases tensions built up during the day that would ordinarily disrupt sleep, and so encourages deep, restful sleep.

Regular practice of the body scan develops a sensitive awareness of one's physical and emotional condition. It releases energy that has been stored in the body, often for long periods of time, that might take the form of stress, illness, or disease. Variations on the technique are used in stress and pain management clinics, and in a wide range of holistic healing approaches. It also teaches us to monitor and release tension as it arises, prevent the build-up of new stress, and heighten body ease and vitality. The practice creates an equanimity and inner poise that allow you to process automatic emotional reactions promptly and respond appropriately to challenging situations with courage and compassion. The greater sensitivity to energy puts you in more direct touch with the inherent enthusiasm and fulfillment of your true nature.

Intuition

Be still and know . . . —Psalms 46:10

I was brought up in a household where extrasensory perception was an ordinary occurrence in everyday life. My father was a natural-born psychic who engaged in it as a hobby his whole life, and for many years practiced it professionally. While I knew he was "different," still it all seemed quite normal to me: that one can read another's thought, or get premonitions of the future, or just know what to do. He told me that everything is consciousness and that all individual minds are joined in the One Mind, which is unobstructed by time and space in its communication with all its apparent forms. Universal consciousness communicates through and with the individual mind, just as neurotransmitters carry messages between the brain and cells of the body, or lasers of light carry e-mail through the server to each desktop, and back again.

Our understandings of the flow of intelligence in a whole system may help to erode the cultural taboo developed by rational, logical, scientific thought against the mystical, intuitive mode of knowing. In the current awakening of consciousness, there is a growing recognition that intuition is a capacity we all have and a legitimate form of knowing. As we open to it, it serves its natural function of revelation and guides us through the mystery.

The word intuition derives from the Indo-European *teu,* which means "to pay attention, to turn to," and the Latin *intueri*: "to look at or toward, contemplate, to watch or protect." Its most recent predecessor in our language is from the Middle English *intuycion,* which meant "contemplation." The root meaning here is the knowing that comes from turning within.

We can define intuition as the act or faculty of direct, immediate knowing without the use of rational or logical processes. It comes in mental, emotional, spiritual, or physical forms that give us direct access to deeper consciousness, to the unknown, to creativity, inspiration, and divine guidance. It's our best means of getting in touch with ourself, or more precisely, the way the Self knows itself.

Intuition happens to all of us at one time or another, even though we often don't recognize it for what it is. It is widely used by business people and leaders who have to act decisively in situations of high ambiguity. It is indispensable for working with uncertainty and insufficient information, or for that matter, with an overwhelming amount of undigested information that takes too long to process solely through rational analysis. Ironically, the current explosion of infinitely expanding information actually means we have comparatively less information available, and thus we have an even greater need to trust our own judgment. In times of rapid change in markets, politics and technology, intuition may be the quickest guide to action once the deadline is upon us.

In business, major decisions are made by "following a hunch" or "going with the gut." Many business people, though, are reluctant to acknowledge that they use intuition since it doesn't conform to the acceptable, hardball decision-making process based on data, reason, and logic. Still, many business executives have been called "extroverted intuitives," who use intuition actively in their daily life and work. Leaders and managers could certainly benefit from tapping into their inner resources and wisdom, as well as from finding the calmness needed in crises or stressful situations. Intuition is an essential part of shaping a vision of new possibilities, stimulating creativity and innovation, hiring, choosing customers, knowing when to abandon ineffective strategies, even investing and determining mergers and acquisitions.

My personal experience and study of intuition reveal that it comes through three primary channels: through the mind, the body, and synchronistic circumstances.

It appears in the mind as insight, hunches, visions, dreams, hearing voices or sounds, the creative "ah ha!" of a sudden solution or brilliant inference. It brings an awareness of how things fit together, a glimpse of the big picture. When highly developed in this way, it's often called extrasensory perception, clairvoyance, telepathy, and precognition, or simply revelation..

When it comes through the body and related feelings, intuition appears as physical sensations, energy rushes, subtle or powerful emotions, empathy, or even pain. The story is told of Einstein who, when developing equations at the blackboard, could tell he was off track by the pain in his back. It is fascinating, with respect to "gut feelings," that research in psychoneuroimmunology has shown that there are receptors in the intestines that receive neurotransmitters from the brain. Gut feelings may truly be the buzzing of our cellular beepers that vibrate when a call comes in from central intelligence!

Intuition also comes through synchronistic occurrences in which seeming coincidences or fortuitous events reveal a deeper pattern of meaning—for example, the underlying unity of life—or the presence of divine guidance. We call it synchronicity when we bump into friends exactly when we need them, or when we randomly open the page of a book and our eyes fall immediately on the message that answers a pressing question. In the unity of existence there are no accidents, as long as we understand that the universe does not exist to do our will.

Intuition has become very important to me personally. While it remained latent for most of my life, despite my father's early influence, I now experience intuition frequently. It is increasingly my main way of responding to the flow of life. Whenever I have to make tough decisions, my choice has to feel right, regardless of what my rational understanding says about it.

My process usually begins with the standard logical approach. I gather all the information I can, think through the pros and cons rationally, consider the arguments, make lists of options and possible outcomes. Then I just sit with it meditatively. I visualize different possible outcomes, alert to what may show up in the picture and how I experience it in my body. I focus first on one outcome and feel the sensations, usually in my chest. Then I focus on another possible outcome and go into it the same way. Sometimes I get constricted, tense, tight, or lethargic feelings. Sometimes I get elation, relief, energy. I go with that. I have used this method in countless examples and have no regrets.

Often the "answer" doesn't come right away. In those cases I admit that I don't know what to do and delegate the question or decision to the unconscious, trusting that something will bubble up at the appropriate time. So I take my mind off it, do other things, and see what comes. The desired insights do indeed bubble up, often to my discomfort, in the middle of the night or on the exercise bike. So I have taken to carrying either a notepad or a voice-activated mini-cassette recorder to capture the fleeting insight before it is gone. I am starting to suspect there is some inverse relationship between heightened intuition and memory loss. Perhaps the willingness to be empty and not retain or accumulate "knowledge" keeps the vessel open and receptive to receiving the flow of insight and guidance.

A growing number of books, some of them listed in my bibliography, give helpful information on how to cultivate the ability to live and work more intuitively. For now, here is a simple process for turning within to heed the inner voice:

Because intuition generally comes unbidden, when you're not "trying," it is essential to develop a quiet, alert receptivity. This is a real challenge for most people, whose continual mind-chatter drowns out the possibility of intuition. The tools already discussed in this chapter provide ways of cultivating this receptivity. The essence of the approach is:

1. Relax your body. Let yourself be. Release the grip, the contraction, the effort, the trying. In a way, it's like going to sleep while awake. You let go of the world, your mind, your body, and just be.

2. Be quiet and listen. Let mental activity subside and observe the silence between your thoughts. The knowing comes through silent awareness.

3. Surrender. Give up the need to maintain control. Give up all in-

tention, all individual effort. Be willing to not-know. While this may get scary, going through the fear of losing control opens you to a deeper knowing and true security. This means giving up the attachment to being an individual who has to do something, to get something, to know something. A culture based solidly on individualism has the enormous challenge of surrendering its belief in the all-powerful individual "I." Intuition is the knowing that shows up when we relinquish the "I-thought" and stay awake. The deepest spirituality calls for this surrender to the larger process, the higher power whose guidance we seek.

We can see the process of intuition from two points of view simultaneously. In the dualistic framework, the individual mind becomes the receptor, the channel and translator of the creativity and wisdom of the universal Self. It benefits from this wisdom and uses it in its drive toward self-actualization and self-transcendence. In the non-dual realization, where the "I" falls away, it is revealed that you *are* the knowing, rather than merely the person who receives the intuition. Here knowing, knower, and known are one and the same. Intuition is the way consciousness knows itself, the way that the universal Self participates consciously as an individual in the world of action.

At the 1996 Intuition Network Conference, which I attended, intuition specialists from around the world addressed many serious questions about intuition: Does it indeed come from God or the divine within us, or merely from the unconscious ego? Is it really a reliable insight, or does it just express an emotional upset or a fear? Can it be used for egotistical, self-serving uses? Is it appropriate to encourage others to use it when we don't know what their motivations are—or when we know their bottom-line motivations are probably crass or greedy? When should we share an intuition of our own openly and actively, and when just be subtle and facilitate others' understanding to get the intuition on their own? Do we need to be clear about our intentions in using intuition? Is intuition always right? Do we use the knowledge that comes from it to manipulate others and influence outcomes? How can we avoid spiritual materialism, as the egoic mainstream tries to take the subtlest of the subtle and turn it to the purposes of sustaining individual greed, all in the name of spiritual purpose?

In response, the experts suggested several precautions and possible solutions to these issues. First, practitioners of intuition must take full responsibility for themselves. You have to be genuinely loving in your motivation, and brutally honest with yourself about any wandering from or corruption of that motivation. When expressing an intuition to others, let them know that what you see is a possibility, not a certainty. Always use intuition in the service of human harmony, realizing that intention is everything. Honor the silence fully and trust that the absolute integrity of your soul will not be unethical. Take the attitude of "Thy will be done" and remain humble in the presence of the supreme power as a constant guard against egotistical inflation. Simply be honest about the way you work intuitively, and do the best you can. Trust that what genuinely comes from the source unfolds perfectly, including any corrections you need along the way.

Silence

The experience of silence alone is the real and perfect knowledge.
—Ramana Maharshi

Throughout this book, I have referred often to the crucial role of silence. It is the key to intuition, to listening, to humility. It is the doorway to both actualization and transcendence. It is the most profound, and yet the most simple and practical of tools for the conscious workplace. Silence can show up at work in many ways. I am beginning more of my one-on-one and group sessions with a few moments of silence as a way for people to "arrive," relax, let go of the previous meeting, and be present to our task. We also use it in preparation for certain self-reflective exercises or to collect our thoughts before a group dialogue. I find that more and more people appreciate the practice for these simple benefits alone.

In a more subtle way, silence shows up at work in the willingness to be quiet when we have nothing to say. It is reflected in our openness to new ideas, our wish to clean out the accumulated encrustation of older ways, theories, premises, to be empty and allow creativity to arise. It is supported by developing a workplace culture that encourages people to admit they might not always be right, to not have easy answers to everything, to realize that it's okay to be wrong and to admit it. In that organizational silence a new voice can arise, new visions can appear, innovation and new directions can occur.

Initially, we may experience silence as the absence of sound. It is quiet, peaceful, a big relief. We love, it, we seek it. It is a clear contrast to the noise of our life and the chatter of everyday mind.

So we cultivate it, make it a practice. We learn to let go of thoughts and focus on the silent spaces between them. Here we find peace. In listening to the silence, I saw clearly that I don't have to quiet the mind or restrain thinking: The silence between the thoughts pulls on me with the force of a black hole. It has a magnetic attraction that generates in me a willingness, a yearning, to listen more deeply, to yield to it, to be immersed in it. It's like making love with silence, both a full embrace of it and a surrender to it. This listening is consciousness turning to itself, sensing the gravitational pull it has on itself, calling itself home.

It is wonderful, yet we may start to judge our efforts when we have noisy, busy thoughts. Then we think we're not doing it well, we are not quiet. You discover you cannot *make* yourself quiet. The quiet is already *here*. You begin to notice that as you dwell in the quiet space between the thoughts, it expands and deepens. You see it is really space—inner space, outer space are the same all-pervasive context—the emptiness in which everything exists. The infinite space in which the planets and galaxies exists, in which all universes exist, is the same space in which all mental activity comes and goes. This space is silence.

The magnificence of this silence allows for everything—sound, thought, and action—to occur within it. Thoughts take place in the silence. They come and go, and the silence is always here, just as the sky is the context for weather. Weather comes and goes. It's the transient, changing, ephemeral. Silence is the unchanging, the timeless. Like empty space, it is qualityless.

Then you realize that silence is the source out of which everything arises, abides in, and to which it returns. It's the formless underlying essence that is constantly giving birth to form—thought, voice, sound—

like the ocean forever giving birth to waves. Ever changing, the waves arise from the ocean, are always the expression of the ocean, and when they return to the ocean they have gone nowhere. Wave and ocean are one. Silence, thought, and activity are one. Silence is not some passive antithesis to action and thought, but the ever-present spacious background of active life.

Finally, you realize that nothing obstructs this silence, that thought is no disruption of your silent Being. You see that all thought arises in this ocean of silence and does not disturb it. Why should the ocean mind if it has waves, if it is turbulent or smooth? The depths are unaffected by the surface.

So live from the depths of silence and enjoy the surface activity without clinging. Love the entire activity of our humanness, our thoughts, feelings, physical experiences. Allow them as expressions of our deep true nature which is always clear and unstained. In this silent being-awareness is the pure knowing that knows itself.

Being Awareness

Attention to one's own Self, which is ever shining, the one undivided and pure reality, is the direct, infallible means to realize the unconditioned, absolute being that you really are.

—Ramana Maharshi

Most meditation techniques focus attention on an object. We are encouraged to concentrate on breath, thoughts, phrases, images, feelings, physical sensations or actions. While these methods are relatively useful, they all reinforce belief in the existence of a separate meditator and ultimately sustain the illusory subject-object split. They come from, and strengthen, the concept that there is a separate individual seeking realization, fulfillment, wholeness, or some other ultimate goal. At some point in this search it becomes clear—if you are fortunate—that the belief in a seeker practicing to get somewhere *is itself the obstacle* to the direct knowing of who you are and always have been.

In this clarity, the individual "I" recognizes the need for its own dissolution. While from the egoic point of view it seems as if practice enables you to attain the unitive wisdom, at the threshold of awakening you intuit that practice exists primarily to exhaust the striving of the separative "I." In giving this up, your true nature is revealed.

The Advaita (non-dual) tradition as taught by Ramana Maharshi and H.W.L. Poonja sees through the appearance of the separate individual to the underlying undivided reality. They advise us to turn awareness back upon the apparent seeker itself, to face the "I" that thinks it is meditating. Ask the ultimate question "Who am I?", focus attention on this "I," and trace it back to its source. Where does this "I" come from? Where does the "I-thought" that sustains separation come from? The point is not to come up with some intellectual answer, but rather to turn your face directly to yourself.

This describes a subtle shift in attention. Rather than looking at the objects of awareness, you turn consciousness back upon itself and *become aware of being aware.* Rather than focusing on thoughts, you focus on the knower of the thoughts, on the conscious subject rather than on the perceived objects, on the seeing rather than on the seen. *When awareness looks upon itself, the split between an observing subject and an observed object disappears.* Face the seeker and the seeker dissolves. Turn to the questioner and the answer is present as your own nature. There is just awareness aware of itself. Instantly there arises the joy of self-recognition, the bliss of freedom. You return to the source of all thought, of all seeking and looking, the source from which identity, subject and object originate. This source is you. Here is the Self that you have always been, the eternally abiding presence, our silent undivided being.

In this grace, you see that all practice and survival strategies were nothing more than the play of consciousness. When you awaken from the dream, it is clear that no one has gone anywhere or attained anything, that the entire process of what we call practice *was* the dream. No one is meditating, no one is declaring, no one is visualizing, no one is intuiting. All of it is the play of the Self.

The awareness that recognizes itself as source-consciousness is pure, unmediated knowing. *"I am that I am"* is the self-intuition of being-awareness that knows that it is. This is not some "other," but what we are, the awake substrate within everything. You cannot know this through mind because mind cannot understand or grasp its source. It can only bow to it in silence. When the individual wave-consciousness turns fully to face itself, it is revealed that you are and always have been the ocean, and that all waves—thoughts, feelings, sensations, actions—are the projections of your own consciousness. In the mystery that all is You, the sought-for freedom and joy is here and now.

> *Find out what is the foundation of Consciousness. Undress the concept of 'I' and jump into the ocean of Existence-Consciousness-Bliss. You are That. You must look to your Self right now. Don't postpone.*
> —Poonjaji

VII

FREEDOM IN THE FLOW OF WORK

Freedom in the Balance

How, then, can we live out the realization of our true nature in our daily work? I have come to see that we can discover our freedom at work in the subtle balance of being and doing. This balance allows us to do our best while sustaining our awareness, fulfillment, and well-being. It is a way of being fully engaged in work while simultaneously being detached from it, of being wholeheartedly present and skillfully involved while not being caught in it. We can be attentive to the minutia of detail and yet see through it all with a liberating transcendental vision. It is a way to take responsible, committed action and yet flow at one with the whole. I want to share my discovery of this freedom and how it can be lived in the day-to-day process of making our full contribution at work.

The Split

For many years I struggled with the fundamental dualism that afflicts many seekers on the spiritual path—the split between the "inner" work on one's spiritual development and the "outer" work of family and making a living.

After twenty-five years of study and practice in the non-dual tradition, I should have known better. I knew theoretically that inner and outer are not really separate, that all dualities are expressions of a single underlying reality which is the source and essence of all things. If all is one, if there is only the universal Self, then everything is the activity of the totality. In reality there is no split between subject and object, between the doer of the work and the work being done. Yet this remained an intellectual concept for me, something I could verbalize quite well but did not actually *live* as my day to day experience. I continued to hold this separation in consciousness, and so experienced the pain of that division and the burning need to find integration.

I left my first job, a comfortable position teaching history at Cornell University, in 1973 to pursue my spiritual studies and practice full time. After five years in the egoic battleground of academics, I was convinced that I could not find well-being or self-realization in the highly competitive Ivy League environment. Exhausted by my own stress, ambition, and perfectionism, I walked away from a well-paying and secure situation for the journey into the unknown. This journey involved twenty-five years of study and practice of meditation, yoga, and other disciplines with recognized world masters, including two years of intensive Zen training with Joshu Sasaki Roshi, and immersion in a wide range of personal growth work with accomplished teachers. While this all certainly benefitted me in many ways, it also paradoxically reinforced the dualistic split.

I had made a clear distinction between the corrupt world and the purity of simple life. I felt compelled to live in the woods, to get away from the money economy and civilization, to live simply, and find the inner purity. For seven years I lived without remunerative work. For a few years I lived on my savings in an idyllic cabin in the woods, without running water and electricity, and with only wood heat. I began to practice meditation and studied the wisdom classics. Then I moved into a similarly rustic rural commune with a strong commitment to meditation and love, in which all work was pure service to the community.

There I tasted for the first time the possibility of true integration in work: work that serves a higher purpose, that reflects my deepest vision and beliefs, that is an act of surrender and devotion. This was not work as I had known it before. My time of service, of logging and splitting firewood, carpentry and house construction, gardening and cooking, was all a delightful dance of joy. It was real relationship with friends I loved and enjoyed working with. It was a natural expression of who I am, my abilities and preferences. In truth it was play, and I often felt deep gratitude for this great luck.

Then in 1980, as the meditation center dissolved, my wife and young daughter and I returned to town and I re-entered the mainstream work world again to "make a living." In the process of building up a successful training, consulting, and leadership coaching business, the old survival concerns and submerged dualistic split arose again. While I was committed to my work as a spiritual practice—seeing it as meditation and service to others—the stresses and anxieties I thought I had left behind came back. I needed regular breaks from work in periodic yoga and meditation retreats in order to experience the sense of wholeness, peace, and well-being I knew to be my true nature. The depth of these retreat experiences just intensified the burning demand to have greater harmony between work and myself.

The Koan of Freedom at Work

In Zen training the master gives the student a koan to meditate on, a mysterious, paradoxical question, such as "What is the sound of one hand clapping?" The question, which has no conceptual answer, is designed to shatter the mind's intellectual hold and reveal, in the silence of no-mind, intuitive knowing. The burning koan I held in my life as I ran my consulting business was: *How can I be fully engaged in work and yet be free? How can I be immersed in the day to day life of family, work, friends, in the midst of an active, urban environment, and be fully awake? How can I handle the endless details and pressures of responsible life and remain centered, peaceful, open, and loving?* All my preaching and wise sayings were worthless without this ultimate realization.

In 1990 my oldest friend on the spiritual path, Lal Gordon, told me of an Indian master who was teaching exactly what I was looking for: fully awakened freedom in the midst of daily life. H.W.L Poonja, an active, well-educated professional man and mining engineer in India, was enlightened in 1947 through his teacher Ramana Maharshi, and continued after his transformation to work for a living to support his large family. Poonjaji—or Papaji, "dear father," as he is called by his many students worldwide—was offering the teaching freely to all comers in the busy, noisy, commercial city of Lucknow in northern India.

Frankly, I was not interested in a guru. I had already had many spiritual teachers in my life. Throughout it all, I was especially drawn to paths that emphasize self-reliance. I was not looking for someone to surrender to and follow. Of course, I have had a lifetime of stubbornness, arrogance, and resistance to authority and control. While it was all in the name of independence, it also masked a fear of love, intimacy, and vulnerability. Only later I realized that it was this proud tendency itself that sustained the painful separation from my own true self and reinforced the distinction between spirit and work. This rebel simply refused to surrender—unless, of course, there was something very big in it for me.

On September 21, 1991, I followed my deepest intuitive urge, sensing that there was something very big for me here. I wrote Papaji: "Can you teach me how to live fully awake and free as Who I Am within the context of my family life and my commitments to support the family through my professional activities as a trainer and consultant?"

To my astonishment, three weeks later I received his handwritten letter in which he gave a resounding yes, invited me to visit him in India, and affirmed:

> You are invited to go here whenever you have convenience. Whenever the desire for freedom arises in a certain mind, it has to be given preference to be attended to right at the same moment, lest this flame may not at all show itself. That is the instant one has to dive within you to find out the Source of this Inner Consciousness. Ask a question to your Self: "Who Am I?" Hold on to the "I," look for from where the "I" rises. Proceed further, make no effort, don't carry alongside any intention, ideation or notion. One need not disturb his routine of life-family-wife-sons-daughter. . . . First you will find your own Self and later you will find the Self seated in all beings.

I finally met Poonjaji in India on March 23, 1992. He was in his early eighties. He had no ashram, accepted no money, lived simply in a plain house, and met with his students in an ordinary neighborhood on the outskirts of the city. He called for no devotion, no followers, and cultivated no attachment to his person. His entire focus was on sharing the simple way to liberation, and his greatest joy was for you to get it and return to your life. Many of his students were westerners who were attracted to him as I was, precisely because his promise was freedom with no strings attached. His daily *satsang* (Sanskrit: "in the company of truth")—sitting, teaching, dialoguing, telling stories, joking with his students—could not have been more integrated in everyday life. As we spoke together, the din of honking traffic and street noise, laughing, shouting schoolchildren, vendors hawking their wares, and barking dogs was always in the background.

In the midst of all this I asked him again how I could be free and awake in the midst of a busy work life, without running away from anything. He laughed and said there was no problem with that. "Just be quiet and don't think." I only needed to take five seconds of my time here and now, a full five seconds without thinking or mental activity of any kind, and he would take me somewhere that would last a lifetime. Being very literal-minded, I took him at his word, and sat there quietly, staring for a while into his eyes, then closing mine and experiencing peace, joy, darkness and light, very normal experiences in my regular meditations. He then asked what I experienced, and when I described it, he said, laughingly, "Good job, you are an honest man."

Papaji joked most of the time, and I figured he was putting me on—there were no bright lights, no energy experiences, no visions, ego was still here. He said he was sure I "got" it and asked me if I were sure. I said, "If you're sure, then I'm sure." Of course, I wasn't sure about anything, except that he was playing with me. But he insisted: "I strike you when the iron is hot. The iron is ready, I am the hammer, and now I strike. You will not lose this, you will not forget this, I'm sure." He said all I needed to do was to take five seconds a day to be quiet and not think. That would be more than sufficient. The Self would do it all.

I asked how I could do my work and not think. It seemed impossible. He said my work comes from the source itself, which is beyond all mental activity. All the energy I need to work is coming from that place. Just come to the inner silence in which the "I" disappears into the True Self, which is doing all the work.

Papaji explained to another student: "Spontaneous activity does not need to be manipulated by intellect, mind, or senses. Spontaneous activity will be conducted by a higher power and it is not your concern! If you are concerned, there is doership, and then karma and the world reappear. To become a doer—"I am doing" —you become responsible. But when you return to discover where this doership arises from, it will leave you. Then some unforeseen, indescribable activity will take charge of you. Unexplainable knowledge will take charge of you. Supreme activity, unheard of, will take charge of you. That is spontaneous activity within itself, and you are not in charge.

"Always, it is your true nature," he continued, "the Self, the unknown, which is responsible for the activity, but the ego claims it. . . . You have to surrender to that supreme unknown emptiness and function from there."

Papaji described his own experience of this automatic flow of work after his awakening when he continued to work as a mining engineer and held other jobs as well to support his family: "In the first few months after my realization, I didn't have a single thought. I could go to the office and perform all my duties without ever having a thought in my head. . . . Everything I did was performed without any mental activity at all. There was an ocean of inner silence that never gave rise to even a ripple of thought. It did not take me long to realize that a mind and thought are not necessary in the world. When one abides as the Self, some divine power takes charge of one's life. All actions then take place spontaneously, and are performed very efficiently, without any mental effort or activity."

Entering the Stream

During the next five years, which included six return visits to India to be with Papaji, I had countless experiences of the mysterious flow of work. I can not explain this, except to say this much: in the willingness to be quiet and turn inward to face the Self, it is clear that there is no separate doer independent of the totality. In the silent absorption of no-thought, the sense of separate individuality falls away and there is the realization of being a timeless presence. It is all just happening in the here and now. In this full engagement, the individual becomes an opening through which the underlying being-awareness-energy flows. The bodymind moves intuitively, harmoniously responsive within the wider whole, as mentioned in the description of "flow" in chapter two.

I found myself living a grand mystery: living proactively as the individual actor, while simultaneously witnessing the flow unfold by itself; being fully engaged in my work while continually surrendering to the stillness in which everything is happening; having an active, creative mind, while returning over and over again to the silence of no thought; working with passion and energy while abiding fulfilled and detached.

For the most part I would simply be aware of the action taking place, observing this bodymind package do everything I did before: give a seminar, make phone calls, seek clients, speak to groups, go in and out of airports, rental cars, and hotels, much of it happening effortlessly, as in a dream. The greatest epiphanies came in this work of making a living. The airport, the conference room, the hotel lobby, the corporate office became my temples; clients and workshop participants became my fellowship and satsang.

My direct experience of the mysterious flow of work is best expressed in these journal entries I made in the weeks following the intense awakening in India in 1992:

> 4-7-92: Ithaca: Now all the information is clear and obvious and easy to communicate. Before, the information was good, yet totally conceptual, coming from memory of past realizations. Now it is wisdom coming from this present Being/Knowing state. The work is just expressing this state. Trust this. It is all done. Work is taking care of itself.
>
> Living free and awake functionally in the world is amazing. Had a $2000 job canceled yesterday. Had been counting on the money to pay the IRS and get through April. Had a moment of disappointment, slight upset, then it was gone. There is such a deep, easy acceptance of what comes. Equanimity is the way of being of the Self in the world: a balanced acceptance of whatever comes, pleasure or pain, benefit or loss.
>
> Giving the *Transforming Stress* seminar today at Cornell, I am

Emptiness: peaceful, open, fully present and relaxed, truly able to see and hear people clearly. Everything is so vividly clear, there is such a deep, quiet joy pervading me. The people are so beautiful, and troubled too. I see their minds in their faces. My responses are coming automatically without effort. I have no idea whether they are "correct" or not. It all sounds okay.

This seminar is very different from past seminars. Although the information is basically the same, it is much more streamlined and direct, more to the point with less verbiage. I listen and let people talk more. Much bliss comes up when I close my eyes, seeing into the golden light. I feel a little stress in the back, some holding in the stomach: comes from making even the slightest effort, or perhaps from some attachment to results. How can I do this totally effortlessly without stress? Let the Self do it all. "I" am not doing anything. Remember the Self each moment. It is real, it is all. Seeing how automatically the seminar flowed through me as an instrument gives more confidence in this process. The Self is truly doing it all. That is what I am. This is all there is and ever has been.

4-8-92: Ithaca: I see too that the work wants, indeed, demands to be done, and that I feel best when I just move forward and do it, rather than trying to return to the bliss through cultivating stillness. Bliss comes when it comes. Remember, I chose the activity of being Free in the midst of family and work. So none of this is a distraction. In fact, surrendering to the activity allows the bliss to be there without effort. The great emptiness and peace and the golden light is always the background and context of all activity. No one is doing anything and it is all getting done. Egolessness dances perfectly in the manifestation. Watch the movie and enjoy! Thank you God, thank you Papaji.

My work is getting clear here. I teach people how to relate, act, accomplish in the manifestation, how to demonstrate and manifest freedom and love in the world and make it work on a nitty-gritty practical level: how to deal with their minds, emotions, etc., for maximum effectiveness, skillfulness, well-being, success. It is about being appropriate, coming from emptiness-being-compassion and expressing it appropriately in life, work, relationships, organizations. It is so simple and clear.

4-10-92: Ithaca: Today I led another full-day seminar at Cornell. I was filled with a joyful, exuberant energy that carried me effortlessly through the day. I experienced myself as pure awareness and presence. What an amazing experience to witness from the place of emptiness a seminar being given by nobody at all. Witnessing the words flowing from this mouth, the responses to peoples' questions, the effortless movement of the body from the board to the chair, what perfection. Every bit of it is channeled through this empty space that I am. God is doing it all, and what a job.

People enjoyed the seminar and gave very positive feedback. Colleagues who had seen me work before India commented on how much I had changed. Little do they know. One little problem: When the energy gets high and the bliss strong, I want to close the eyes. If I do so, I might disappear without a clue how long I was gone. Not a great idea when I'm leading a workshop to shut my eyes and disappear. It is real work to stay grounded in the manifestation and keep my eyes open and be fully present. When I am fully present there is no distance between us, as if I exist in their space. It is not quite being "one" with them, just that there is no distance or separation. This is new to me now and I will keep trying this out.

4-11-92: Ithaca: My behavior has definitely changed. So much patience, acceptance, and equanimity with people. Yet I am much more direct and speak up easily. I was almost shocked at what I was saying to people in the seminar yesterday. They didn't seem to mind. I am doing none of this. I witness it happening automatically, unconsciously, on its own.

4-27-92: Kansas City: What a sweet, effortless day. Such deep peace, going through the seminar in the elegant Adam's Mark Hotel with 125 people, coming from empty mind, the seminar went by effortlessly, timelessly, as if it is all taking place in a inner

Grand Canyon of infinite quietness, just witnessing, thoughts flying, no thinker. Such stillness as the space of all outer activity. What grace.

5-5-92: Papaji wrote: "Your letter dt 25th April shows you have been very busy after your return from Lucknow, with seminars, showing them how to keep peace while active. I am sure you have known the secret [of] how to keep with people yet not keeping any connection with anyone including your own Self. All the activity is ceaselessly being done thru the Awareness-Being by itself."

5-12-92: Columbia, SC: Totally involved today in the seminar, on automatic, attending to business and details. Amazed at the effortless flow in handling over 175 people in a noisy, crowded conference room with many breakdowns, not enough tables, poor visibility and sound, toilets overflowing, restaurant closed at lunch, etc.

5-13-92: Ithaca: My teaching work has changed as it flows from Self. I stand in the conference room and witness the talking and action pouring out of me spontaneously: emptiness sharing itself as form. Since returning from India I have been to ten different cities around the U.S. and have given more than fifteen seminars to over one thousand people.

Through the last six years, my corporate work changed radically in content and approach. As the experience of freedom continued to unfold, I was more emboldened to share the simple basics of self-realization and the fundamental principles of consciousness within my training and consulting. I have been more selective in the training topics I offer, recently focusing on those topics that serve self-realization more directly—such as retreats on the awakening of leadership, and globalization as an opportunity to discuss unitive consciousness. I have also discovered a greater effectiveness and joy in my one-on-one coaching with leaders. I have been delighted to discover that some of them are just as intent on self-realization as they are on the specific aspects of self-actualization for which they initially approached me.

As we explored deeper possibilities, I realized that the work of awakening is occurring right in the corporate halls and conference rooms. I was amazed to discover the depth of the experience my clients and I were going through, as if we were walking together into the unknown realms of expanding awareness.

It is said that what we call enlightenment is really a process of disillusionment—the stripping away of all illusions of who you are and what is going on until you come to the direct, unmediated knowing of reality. All the expectations I had held about an "experience" to be had in the future in some typical "spiritual" setting were stripped away until I came face to face with the amazing fact that it is all taking place right here in the work setting. I didn't have to leave, I didn't have to sit on a mountain in India or go back to the woods. This was a dream come true that I never quite expected to happen this way, even though I had asked for it. As Papaji said—and I hear his voice often within me—the Self really is doing it all. Just keep quiet and let it happen.

Still, even though the veils parted and revealed the vast expanse of freedom, some doubt or questioning kept creeping back in, some desire to understand this magnificent reality that was happening. My intellectual's mind kept holding it as a conundrum. I wanted to understand and explain to myself and others how I could be the individual and the whole simultaneously, how there could be free will and the seamless, automatic flow of the totality. This became a burning question, a true koan that sat in my stomach like a red-hot iron ball as I struggled to integrate this conceptual paradox.

In the fall of 1997, at the time Papaji passed away at the age of eighty-seven, the grace of resolution came. It took place over a period of two months, part of the time spent in consulting work, part of it during my last month's retreat in India after his cremation. It seemed to be the master's final gift in the mysterious transmission of freedom he offered so wholeheartedly to his students. An awareness dawned as gently and quietly as the morning sun, a knowing without doubt or question that paradox and koan are merely concepts of the egoic mind that point directly to the simplicity of what is.

Balancing Engagement & Detachment

The simplicity of the flow shows up in the balance of being fully engaged and detached simultaneously. For me this starts with Reinhold Niebuhr's famous *serenity prayer*, one of the most profound and useful principles in the world wisdom traditions: "God, grant me the serenity to accept the things I cannot change, the courage to change the things I can, and the wisdom to know the difference."

The prayer presents two polarities of human experience that cover the range of approaches we can take when dealing with any situation or person. The proactive or controlling principle focuses on what you can change, and the flexible or allowing principle accepts what is beyond your control or desire to change. It describes the masculine, assertive yang and the feminine, receptive yin—the two complementary forces that drive the wheel of life. When they are balanced we experience our full effectiveness and freedom in living.

Engagement

The courage to change what you can describes the proactive stand of full engagement in work. For me this involvement required a basic choice to be in the world. From my earliest memories my strongest inherent tendency has always been to withdraw, to not be here, to hang out alone. As a youth I just thought I was anti-social. When I later picked up spiritual understandings, I jokingly mused about the possibility of past lives as a cave yogi. However I want to view it, it has been a supreme challenge for me to choose to be here, that is, to choose to get involved in relationship and play in the manifestation.

To choose our work is freeing. To see that our lives are made up of choices and to honor those choices, releases us from the debilitating victim-mentality of "having to" work. The belief that we "have to" do anything ties up our energy to participate fully. My choice to continue to work has been exhilarating, freeing up great energy to make my contribution. I often have this dialogue with those who think they "have to" work, explaining that choice is the essential underpinning for true self-motivation and responsibility at work. Every piece of work that is delegated to us becomes ours when we choose it. In this sense, we are only working for ourselves.

Our willingness to choose allows us to see, finally and clearly, that this is it. When we get it that this is it, no matter whether we like it or not, we have finally made our peace with reality, and in that surrender, reality adorns and blesses us. As he lay on his death bed, surrounded by his disciples who begged him not to go, the great sage Ramana Maharshi gazed at them compassionately and responded whimsically with his final teaching: "Where could I go?" To choose to be here reveals that here is all there is, and the trap of seeking to be somewhere else just keeps us caught in the seeking. In choice we are home free.

When we choose to be here our attention is freed up as well. We can be awake and present. To be fully mindful in the here and now is the grounding for all effective participation in work and life. The practice of meditation, of mindfulness, of listening releases our energy for successful accomplishment.

Phil Jackson, coach of the Chicago Bulls, arguably one of the greatest teams in the history of basketball, has trained his players in mindfulness practice, the effects of which he describes in his book *Sacred Hoops*:

> Basketball is a complex dance that requires shifting . . . at lightning speed. To excel, you need to act with a clear mind and be totally focused on what *everyone* on the floor is doing. Some athletes describe this quality of mind as a "cocoon of concentration." But that implies shutting out the world when what you really need to do is to become more acutely aware of what's happening right now, *this very moment.*
>
> The secret is *not thinking.* That doesn't mean being stupid; it means quieting the endless jabbering of thoughts so that your body can do instinctively what it's been trained to do without the mind getting in the way. All of us have had flashes of this sense of oneness—making love, creating a work of art—when we're completely immersed in the moment, inseparable from what we're doing. This kind of experience happens all the time on the basketball floor; that's why the game is so intoxicating."

Michael [Jordan] always maintained that he didn't need any of "that Zen stuff" because he already had a positive outlook on life. Who am I to argue? In the process of becoming a great athlete, Michael had attained a quality of mind few Zen students ever achieve. His ability to stay relaxed and intensely focused in the midst of chaos is unsurpassed. He loves being in the center of a storm. While everyone else is spinning madly out of control, he moves effortlessly across the floor, enveloped by a great stillness.

The driving force behind our full engagement in work is commitment. The actual process of commitment embraces many of the qualities discussed in this book. Commitment is both the goal and the steady rechanneling of energy to meet it. It is grounded in vision and impelled by the sheer energy of our enthusiasm. We are most committed when we are passionate about our work, when we are willing to follow our bliss, as Joseph Campbell recommended. Enthusiasm, remember, means filled with *theos,* the divine energy or spirit. As the Roman scholar Tertullian (c.155–c.245) invoked: "Where our work is, there let our joy be."

Commitment is our willingness to take a stand and to be responsible for the result. It is a dynamic expression of our integrity—a promise or pledge to do something. Your word is a powerful force in your life and, as we have seen, a creative act that brings forth new possibilities. Fernando Flores, founder of the Communication for Action workshop, points out that a promise is an action that goes until fulfillment, an ongoing dedication, earnestness, perseverance you live in and renew until it is completed. I often see it as the same energy it takes for a toddler to learn to walk. They stand up, fall down, stand up, fall down. That drive to get back up is commitment.

The big trap in getting so fully engaged, of course, is that we become attached to the outcomes of our activity. That attachment, then, causes our suffering, our stress, anger, and disappointments as we react to the inevitable ups and downs of our involvement. Attachment to desire and fear keeps us locked into the egoic framework and, no matter how successful and effective we are in the area of work, we will never experience ultimate freedom within that framework. The challenge here is to be engaged without being attached, to be fully involved and present, yet at the same time, not caught in the drama.

In his book *The Heart Aroused*, David Whyte wisely points out how engagement and detachment go hand in hand for positive effects at work:

> Preserving the soul means that we come out of hiding at last and bring more of ourselves into the workplace. Especially the parts that do not "belong" to the company. *In a sense, the very part of us that doesn't have the least interest in the organization is our greatest offering to it.* [italics mine] It is the part that opens the window of the imagination and allows fresh air into the meeting room. It is the part that can put the foot on the brake when the organization is running itself off a cliff. It's the part that can identify unethical behavior and remind everyone what the real priorities are. It is the part that refuses to shame itself or others in order to make its way through the organization. In short, its identity is not locked into the fears that stop an organization from having the perspectives and adaptability to save itself.

The key, of course, is to understand and nurture the detachment that frees us to do the right thing.

Detachment

Lao Tzu taught that detachment brings balance. He said that the person who steers clear of deluding entanglements will naturally achieve a balanced state of being that is beyond the influences of love and hate, profit and loss, praise and blame. To live in this way, he taught, is to live the most desirable of lives.

Detachment is a way of holding yourself and life that frees you from being bound by the very conditions you are actively involved in. It is a penetrating awareness at the core of the perennial wisdom that sees through appearances and by its very nature generates liberation.

Because it is a subtle, finely discriminating stand, detachment is often misunderstood. So before describing what it is, it is best to be clear about what it is not. It's not about running away from life, or a kind of aloof emotional withdrawal. Nor is it boredom, coldness, a lack of love or caring for others. In fact, the more we are engaged in life, present and awake, the easier it is to be detached.

Recognition of impermanence

Our detachment is grounded in a clear recognition of the basic impermanence of life. As we look deeply at the reality of change, we see that everything is evolving, moving, expanding, contracting, vibrating, arising and passing away. Life is a continual process of becoming—being born, growing, maturing, decaying, dying. Bucky Fuller liked to remind us that we are a verb, not a noun, best experienced as a flowing stream, not a solid, stationary pebble. The "thingness" of things is created by mind, from the conceptualization which freezes the dynamic movement of flow into apparently fixed entities.

From the perspective of ongoing transformation there are no things, only processes. Here is one meaning of "no-thing-ness": No thing stands still long enough to be anything. Look at the human being: From the moment sperm meets egg until we become ashes and dust, we are in fact a continual process of change. Buddhist wisdom sees in this ongoing flux the reality of selflessness, that there is no such thing as a fixed "self" in the ongoing movement of currents and tendencies. The individual self is nothing more than an idea that freezes the moving stream of tendencies into an appearance of a solid object, held together by memory. To be awake to this underlying emptiness is to detach from the idea of self, from the belief that there is some objective individuality separate from the totality.

In fact, "solid objects" only exist at the most superficial levels of human perception. As western science attests, beneath the surface of the apparent physicality of objects is the reality of continuous molecular composition and decomposition. Within that is the ongoing subatomic activity of particles and wavicles, which are themselves interchangeable forms of the underlying energy. Physicist and student of consciousness Fred Alan Wolf has pointed out that only a tiny part of the atom is mass, and that 99% is space, an emptiness filled with pure potentiality. The basic dynamic insubstantiality of the physical universe is described in the Perennial Philosophy's view that all manifestation arises from the play of intangible energy and consciousness in space.

When we appreciate that our world is constantly changing and insubstantial, we realize that we cannot hold on to that which cannot be grasped. The greatest source of our suffering is trying to hold on to the elusive, ephemeral flow of impermanence. The realization that we cannot cling to the unclingable empowers us to flow with the unpredictable change, uncertainty, and ambiguity of the contemporary workplace. The truly skillful change-masters make their home in this flux and work creatively with the quantum soup of possibilities.

Ralph Waldo Emerson captured this special quality in his *Journals*:

> Nature ever flows; stands never still. Motion or change is her mode of existence. The poetic eye sees in Man the Brother of the River, and in Woman the Sister of the River. Their life is always transitions. Hard blockheads only drive nails all the time; forever . . . fixing. Heroes do not fix, but flow, bend forward ever and invent a resource for every moment.

To "flow, bend forward ever," to flow skillfully with change means that we must become flexible and agile, ready and willing to move in new directions when appropriate. It means holding our desires, attachments, and goals lightly enough so that we can release them and correct our course when new possibilities or the unmovable mountain show up. I often think of it as playing life the way you play your hand in a game of gin rummy. You must be continually rearranging your hand as new cards come into it. It means we are ready to wing it, invent a new resource for each moment. This is the essence of spontaneity and on-the-job learning. We do so by holding things lightly, ready to let go. The most vivid example in my work life recently is my willingness, finally, to use only pencil in recording the ever-changing fluctuations in my scheduling book—after years of insisting on using pen in hopes it would magically prevent cancellations.

Letting go

To detach literally means to let go. There are a number of areas where we must release our grip if we are to experience full freedom at work. The first is to let go of returns and rewards. That is, we come to understand that we do our best work because we are freely choosing to make a difference, not because we are going to get something back. How much of our giving is a veiled attempt at exchange? How much of our output is based on the expectation of getting something in return? Our attachment to praise, reward, recognition locks us into the subtle manipulations that tie up our energy and divert self-motivation toward dependency on external stimulation. While I encourage my clients to praise and reward one another amply, I also caution them not to rely on such things, and to experience their authentic motivation from within. We want to give and we feel best when we give. Albert Schweitzer understood this deep need to share our contribution freely: "The only ones among you who will be truly happy are those who have sought and found how to serve."

I am speaking here of looking at your work as an offering, as a gift with no strings attached. Besides, the value of what you do can never be measured. This is the foundation for true service, which gives because it is needed, because it is appropriate, because it makes a difference. Period. Any subtle manipulation for a return converts it into exchange. The reward is in the giving itself. This is the basis for karma yoga, the Hindu path of service. Like the bodhisattva path in Buddhism or the Judaeo-Christian act of charity, the attention on service turns work into a spiritual act. Working without expectation of return cuts through egoic drives and allows our true nature to emerge.

We can also learn to let go of results. This is particularly challenging in a work culture based on measuring outcomes through high-performance feedback methods, managing by objectives, and quality audits. So what does it mean to be detached from results in a results-oriented, accomplishment-focused society? It does not mean relaxed standards or laggard performance, or the diminishing of your energy and commitment to quality. Fundamentally, it means that you do the very best you can, you give it your best shot, and then you take what you get.

You accept the results, be it success or failure, with equanimity.

Papaji, who continued to work for a living in various professional and business roles long after his awakening, advised us: "Do your work with no expectations for the results. They are not in your hand. Someone else decides the result. Your responsibility is to perform activities which are needed to your standard and not to [attach to] results. . . . This will give you happiness."

It is difficult in our measurement-oriented mentality to understand that there is no automatic one-to-one causality between effort and result. That is, in the realm of human creativity, input does not necessarily guarantee output. You may have done everything you could and it still didn't work out as planned. There are too many variables to be in control of the outcome. Still, so many people are caught in measuring their validity and worth according to their accomplishments.

The key here is to disentangle your sense of identity from your achievements. Sooner or later you must see that your being is not dependent on doing, that your worth or fulfillment is not dependent on whether you succeed or fail, on how much you produce or how much money you make. Detachment here means letting go of stress-producing perfectionist and workaholic tendencies, and realizing that happiness or satisfaction does not come from doing. This is a massive challenge to the deeply ingrained Puritan work ethic that subliminally believes in salvation through accomplishment. We are saved from this exhausting treadmill when we remember that the Kingdom of Heaven is within us. Only within can we find that which is not dependent on anything.

Deeper than actions and words is silent being, where we are already satisfied and fulfilled, inherently whole and at one with life. Here freedom and joy are present and complete, not dependent on the daily ups and downs of work and organizational life. As we come to know the fullness of being, we can rest assured that whether or not we reach our vision or accomplish our goals, it is enough just to be.

We can be detached from returns and results when we have tasted our true nature. Without that taste of real knowing, we keep seeking outside and remain locked into the survival strategies of desire and fear. Papaji used to tell us: "You are an emperor, not a beggar. All the treasure of the universe is within you. Don't beg for anything." The reassurance of the masters allows us to let go of the continual pull of desire. "You are the infinite potentiality, the inexhaustible possibility," the great Indian sage Nisargadatta Maharaj would tell his students. "Because you are, all can be. The universe is but a partial manifestation of your limitless capacity to become."

It takes only one glimpse of this limitless abundance to understand that fulfillment does not come from gratifying our desires, but rather, from abiding in the desirelessness that exists prior to all seeking and aversion. This is the awareness that witnesses the coming and going of desire and fear without attachment, that is not pulled to pursue the survival payoffs. When we are no longer engaged in the struggle for survival, we discover that happiness and satisfaction are aspects of our original nature.

This awareness allows us to transform our desires into preferences and reduce them to the critical few. In our patience and satisfaction we find that the universe offers us delightful surprises. We accept and enjoy what is given when it is here and do not cling to it when it is gone. We allow happiness and sadness, success and failure, gain and loss to come and go.

The wealth of our underlying well-being is ours when we don't hold on to what comes and goes: Paradoxically, in grasping at the ephemeral, we rob ourselves of the timeless. Zen Master Joshu Sasaki Roshi used to tell us that enlightenment is simply the full and total embrace of your karma, that is, the unconditional acceptance of your experience of life.

Equally challenging is the demand to let go of knowing. As mentioned in the discussion of intuition, as more information is available to us, we realize that we know less and less about more and more. On the one hand, I would say this is priming our consciousness to recognize the infinite. On the other hand, it means we must be willing to operate with increasing awareness of our ignorance and make decisions comfortably, knowing that we do not have all the information—or that the data, markets, economic systems, etc., are changing so rapidly that we are basically winging it anyway. Giving yourself permission not to know is especially challenging in a left-brain, rational, scientific culture proud of the intellect as its primary way of understanding and shaping life. Your sense of competence may be threatened until you realize the wisdom and value of not-knowing.

Here not-knowing means cultivating the "beginner's mind," which is open and receptive to constant and rapid change. The incredible burst in creativity and innovation in science and technology, business practices, and organizational forms means we cannot hold on to old ideas and ways of doing things. We need to develop a nimble, agile mind that does not cling to the known, that can let go of old assumptions and models, that is flexible and alert to adjusting to the new. It calls for listening attentively to life and ourselves. We cultivate a situational mindfulness that closely observes life to detect emerging patterns and possible directions of the flow. In the quiet presence, intuition becomes our guide.

Our willingness to not know is fully consistent with the understanding that the ultimate wisdom arises in the silence of no-thought. "Only Don't Know," is the main teaching of the Korean Zen Master Seung Sahn, not only because our original nature shines freely in the absence of mental activity, but also because the empty, quiet mind sees clearly and responds appropriately to life. Not-knowing—an alert clarity not to be confused with blankness or dullness—is the doorway to a deeper knowing.

It is also ironic that computers and information systems, with their ability to store and retrieve massive amounts of information, literally give us greater opportunity to remain quiet and empty. As long as we know how to find the information, we don't have to hold the knowledge. I've also been musing about the possible correlation between the expanding size of computer memory and the correspondingly rapid memory loss I have been experiencing lately!

Of course, all of this letting go—of returns, results, knowing—brings us face to face with the need to let go of control. Our desire for control is a psychological drive, not a true prerequisite for success. But we will never know that until we let go and discover for ourselves the freedom that exists beyond our need for control. Control is an egoic survival strategy that may initially serve our quest for self-actualization, but becomes a key obstacle to self-transcendence. It is the mind's strategic reaction to fear, our fear of not getting our way, of losing, failing, not getting there, being overwhelmed or rendered weak and helpless. The vicious cycle of fear and control blocks our freedom.

Trust & Surrender

We can release our fear-driven, white-knuckled grip on control by trusting. I define trust in various ways along a spectrum of expanding self-awareness and identity. At the most basic, egoic level, trust is the belief that everything will work out the way I want. This narcissistic self-centeredness assumes that life exists to do my will. As we mature, we may understand that you can't always get what you want, and so develop a greater trust in ourselves—trust that we have what it takes to handle whatever comes, whether it is to our liking or not. This stand represents a kind of egoic maturity grounded in self-confidence and personal affirmation.

We may also trust that everything happens for the best according to some wider, deeper purpose that we recognize is beyond our egoic survival issues. Whether we call it God's will, the divine plan, providence, the Tao, karma, or destiny, this perspective provides a framework of understanding within which we can relax and let go. We can experience comfort, security, and humility and give ourselves permission to surrender our will to a higher principle.

For many westerners, trust is grounded in our fascination with the idea of progress toward higher states of being. Whether it be the Judaeo-Christian focus on spiritual progress toward salvation, the coming Millenium and the return of the Messiah, or the rational-secular-scientific focus on historical development toward social utopias, technological innovation, and continuous improvement, we seem compelled to view life as a process of becoming, from lower to higher, from less to more. We take comfort in the belief that our life, or history as a whole, is actually leading somewhere desirable.

One recent upgrade of this worship of progress is the current marriage of holism and systems theory in the idea of self-organizing systems. The ascending evolutionary vision sees in life a self-organizing process toward new forms of order, complexity, and consciousness as living systems adapt themselves to the demands of the changing environment. Even periods of disruptive change and disorder—as in our current time of transformation—are seen as crucibles of the transformation toward higher levels of wholeness and order.

The holistic vision of life as an interdependent, networked whole system is another intellectual approach to trust. The sciences of environmental studies and psychoneuroimmunology are fully consistent with the ancient image of the Perennial Philosophy that we are all waves on the ocean of being, each of us a temporary form of the underlying unity. When we know this, how can we not trust? What is to fear when you know you are the whole?

All of these intellectual scaffoldings give us a comfort zone within which to trust and let go. Here mind serves the deep yearning for self-transcendence. The mind is a two-edged sword, both a tool of control and survival of the individual, as well as the architect of the intellectual safety net for our projected surrender. Yet mind can only bring us to the brink. We must then take the plunge into our deepest heart's desire.

As Margaret Wheatley disclosed so poignantly: "I want to stop holding things together. I want to experience such safety that the concept of 'allowing'—trusting that the appropriate forms can emerge—ceases to be scary. I want to surrender my care of the universe and become a participating member, with everyone I work with, in an organization that moves gracefully with its environment, trusting in the unfolding dance of order."

Surrender is the final spiritual act. In the competitive, macho battleground of western culture, surrender has a bad press. It smacks of losing, defeat, weakness, humiliation, passivity. These concerns reflect ego's refusal to dissolve into source, its fear of disappearing. So surrender involves the willingness to feel fear. We must fully embrace the anxiety or terror that may well arise at the very threshold of freedom. To relax entirely and allow the current of fear to pass through you and dissipate is liberating. It shows you that fear is a contraction of your fundamental life energy which can now be experienced in its natural state as joy, what the Hindus call *ananda*, or bliss. Surrender is ecstatic, as the great mystics Rumi, Kabir, and other lovers of the ultimate have shown in their intoxicating poetry. Indeed, once you taste the freedom and sweetness of surrender, you may come to appreciate the declaration of Stephen Nachmanovitch, a musician and student of creativity: "I am not in the music business, I am not in the creativity business; I am in the surrender business."

Full Unemployment in the Flow

One does nothing, and nothing is left undone.—Ram Dass

The ultimate surrender in the non-dual approach is to give up exclusive identification with the "doer." It is the surrender of the I-thought itself, which has been all along the core obstacle to the realization of our self-nature and harmony with the flow.

I remember reading over and over again Ramana Maharshi's response to a questioner who asked if he should renounce his work for spiritual activity:

> The feeling "I work" is the hindrance. Ask yourself, "Who works?" Remember who you are. Then the work will not bind you, it will go on automatically. Make no effort either to work or to renounce; it is your effort which is the bondage.... If you are destined not to work, work cannot be had even if you hunt for it. If you are destined to work, you will not be able to avoid it....
>
> The Self is universal so all actions will go on whether you strain yourself to be engaged in them or not. The work will go on of itself.
>
> Attending to the Self means attending to the work. Because you identify yourself with the body, you think that work is done by you. But the body and its activities, including that work, are not apart from the Self....
>
> What is the undercurrent which vivifies the mind, enables it to do all the work? It is the Self. So that is the real source of your activity. Simply be aware of it during your work and do not forget it. Contemplate in the background of your mind even whilst working. ... avoid haste, which causes you to forget. Be deliberate. Practice

meditation to still the mind and cause it to become aware of its true relationship to the Self which supports it. Do not imagine it is you who are doing the work. Think that the underlying current is doing it. Identify yourself with the current. If you work unhurriedly, recollectedly, your work or service need not be a hindrance.

The flow of work is actually the simplest of experiences. The essence of the Zen realization is sometimes described as "chop wood, carry water." As you carry out your daily tasks fully mindful in the here and now, the "I" dissolves into the dynamic stream of activity. There is no "you" separate from the work process; the work is just happening by itself.

Jean Klein, the Swiss Advaita master, describes the flow: "In action which springs from completeness there's no actor to act, there's only action. You are functioning and the "I" is absent. The moment the "I"-thought comes up, you become self-conscious and caught in conflict. In the absence of this thought there is no speaker or listener, no subject controlling an object. Only then is there complete harmony and adequacy in every circumstance."

In this flow, work becomes a vehicle for freedom: a release from the illusion of separateness. It serves as an altar for the surrender of ego, a place to participate in something beyond oneself, an act of devotion or worship.

I call this full unemployment in the flow of work. Ironically, now that the traumatic experience of downsizing has vividly revealed the illusion of job security in the workplace, we may have the opportunity to find our lasting sanctuary in this spirit of total unemployment. That is, when the "doer" is out of a job—when there is no identification with the individual "I." Then the true work flows effortlessly.

As the song goes, "Freedom's just another word for nothin' left to lose." This is the ultimate value of egolessness. When you act from ego, you are driven by the twin engines of desire and fear, caught in the survival agendas of winning and losing that sustain suffering. When you come from egolessness, then you are here with nothing to lose. From this place of equanimity, you can take the risks you need to take and say what you need to say.

Transcendental wisdom sees through the "I" of doership to the unchanging being that plays all the roles. Here we understand the deeper meaning of Shakespeare's classic dictum: "All the world's a stage and men and women merely players."

To update the metaphor: Awakened consciousness watches the three-dimensional movie of light and form manifesting in space. The movie of life is both projected and received by mind as the instrument of creation. So we simultaneously play and witness our role in our own movie. Being-awareness views the ups and downs of the characters while remaining unaffected, in the same way that the light on the movie screen is never affected by the forms it projects. When there is a fire in the movie, the light or screen does not burn. To dwell as the conscious source beyond it all is pure freedom. It is the ultimate abode, beyond even letting go, trust, and surrender. For in this realization there is no one who needs to take those actions. This wisdom frees us to be here and play the game of work lightly.

Play is a natural energy of the Self that arises spontaneously when we let go of the ballast of egoic concerns and are no longer weighed down by the gravity of our own survival. I love the Hindu interpretation that all life is the divine *lila*—the cosmic play of the supreme Self—enacted for its own enjoyment and entertainment. I would even venture to suggest that the ultimate purpose of life is play—that we are here to enjoy and share love with one another, and in this play to allow our creativity to generate the endless innovation in ideas, technology, products, and service that make up the real outcome of work. Just imagine what the workplace would be like if we followed Frost's suggestion that "work is play for mortal stakes" and fully allowed the joyful spirit of play to infuse our work.

"Play is always a matter of context. It is not what we do but how we do it," Nachmanovitch pointed out. "Creative work is play; it is free speculation using the materials of one's chosen form. . . . The mood of play can be impish or supremely solemn. When the most challenging labors are undertaken from the joyous work spirit, they are play. . . ." Play frees up our energy for our full contribution. Our challenge, then, is to see our work as play, and to allow the lightness of our original nature to radiate through our work and relationships with our co-workers. After all, the root meaning of enlightenment is to lighten up.

I am fortunate now to be able to work with a group of managers who, more often than not, have that twinkle of fun in their eyes. They are exuberant at times and can see their work as play, sometimes high drama. Successful performers often experience their work as a heroic saga, epic adventure, mystery story, inner game, spiritual quest. Whatever the metaphor, it is certainly not humdrum. Realistically, not all jobs readily lend themselves to the light aspects of play. Many of us recently have left jobs or re-defined work and career to be more in harmony with this spirit.

In the flow, qualities and processes that previously seemed to serve the egoic mentality are now seen to be aspects of the unitive consciousness playing itself out as the totality. Commitment, for example, becomes a state of surrender and trust in playing out destiny. As Joe Jaworski aptly describes the shift in his awareness as a leader:

> In my old way of operating, I was very clear about my capacity to commit to something. Commitment meant being highly disciplined in sticking with something. I had been taught early on that the way you win lawsuits is to make it happen—outwork the other person, stick with it, and stay deeply committed to what you are doing. This is the kind of commitment where you seize fate by the throat and do whatever it takes to succeed. It was only later that I began to understand another, deeper aspect of commitment. This kind of commitment begins not with will, but with willingness. We begin to listen to the inner voice that helps guide us as our journey unfolds. The underlying component of this kind of commitment is our trust in the playing out of our destiny. We have the integrity to stand in a "state of surrender," as [Francisco] Varela put it, knowing that whatever we need at the moment to meet our destiny will be available to us. It is at this point that we alter our relationship with the future.

> When we operate in this state of commitment, we see ourselves as an essential part of the unfolding of the universe. In this state of

being, our life is naturally infused with meaning, and as Buber says, we sacrifice our "puny, unfree will" to our "grand will, which quits defined for destined being."

In the same way, when the "I" dissolves into the totality, responsibility takes on its ultimate meaning: the ability to respond appropriately within the larger flow. It reveals to us the mystery of doing and not-doing simultaneously, what the Chinese call wei wu wei, active non-action. The mystery is not resolved intellectually; it is lived, held in the belly and allowed to exist. As the apparent individual, you act with full responsibility, making choices and decisions. Yet you know that the totality—the larger you—is doing it all. As my dharma friend, Lal Gordon told me, "You choose and there is no choice." The traditional debate in western philosophy of "free will versus determinism" is stuck in the either/or thinking of the dualistic framework. From the non-dual point of view, its both/and and neither.

The great Indian Advaita master Ramesh S. Balsekar, a retired bank president and avid golfer, describes this paradox:

> You must act in life *as if* you are the doer, knowing that you are *not* the doer.
>
> The human being lives on fictions. For example, the human being knows that the sun is stationary and that it is the earth that is in movement but nonetheless in his daily life he accepts the fiction that the sun rises and sets.
>
> So the understanding is . . . that you do not have any free will, but in life you must act as if you have free will. . . . So the meaning of *as if* is very clear . . . you have to act. In fact, you cannot *not* act. The body-mind organism must react to an event. You must make decisions and you must make them as if they are your own decisions.
>
> Let your intellectual understanding be that you are not the doer and continue to function as if you are the doer. Over the course of time, this intellectual understanding that you are not the doer will go deeper and all actions that happen will be recognized as spontaneous actions, not "your" actions.

When this "me" itself disappears, then the understanding is of a different nature, then there will be no "me" wanting to do anything. Then whatever happens will happen by itself with the "me" not there.

Here the individual and the whole are seen to be one and the same, and different all at once—two expressions of the indescribable mystery. Sameness and difference are both qualities of being, just as unity includes duality. The many and the one, individual action and flow, the wave and the ocean, this is the dance of That which is doing it all, unfolding itself perfectly. We, as individuals, are the way It manifests as the world. As we participate consciously in this process, we freely enact the boundless creativity of wisdom at work.

ANNOTATED BIBLIOGRAPHY

This is not an an attempt to survey the vast literature on work, leadership, high performance, the Perennial Philosophy and world spirituality, philosophy, psychology, mind-body studies, and holistic health. I list here the writings and authors that have been cited in the text or that were essential to my thinking and inspiration.

American State Papers. No. 43 of *Great Books of the Western World,* edited by Mortimer J. Adler. Chicago: Encyclopedia Britannica, 1952. Contains the Declaration of Independence, U.S. Constitution, and Federalist papers, and writings by John Stuart Mill.

Autry, James. *Love and Profit: The Art of Caring Leadership.* New York: Avon Books, 1991.

————. *Life and Work: A Manager's Search for Meaning.* New York: William Morrow and Co., 1994. Executive and poet Autry reflects on the integration of consciousness and work.

Balsekar, Ramesh S. *Consciousness Speaks.* Edited by Wayne Liquorman. Redondo Beach, CA: Advaita, 1992. Balsekar, a living Advaita master, formerly a successful banker, describes the simplicity of enlightened consciousness.

Bennis, Warren and Burt Nanus. *Leaders: The Strategies for Taking Charge.* New York: Harper & Row, 1986. Succinct study of transformative leadership emphasizing self-management, vision, communication, empowerment, trust, emotional wisdom, positive self-regard.

The Holy Bible. King James Version. New York: American Bible Society.

————. New International Version. Grand Rapids: Zondervan.

Bolan, Lee G. and Terrence E. Deal. *Leading With The Soul: An Uncommon Journey of Spirit*. San Francisco: Jossey-Bass, 1995. Two experts on leadership explore its spiritual dimensions with sensitive insight and practical examples from their research.

Block, Peter. *The Empowered Manager*. San Francisco: Jossey-Bass, 1987. Wise, practical study of how to be empowered in organizations with a graceful balance of political realities, and psychological and spiritual dimensions. An inspiring model that gave me hope such an integration is possible at work.

————. *Stewardship: Choosing Service over Self-Interest*. San Francisco: Berret-Koehler, 1993. Integration of the practical and spiritual aspects of leading organizations today by a savvy consultant, focusing on stewardship, service, partnership, and empowerment as key functions of enlightened leadership.

Brunton, Paul. *The Notebooks of Paul Brunton*, 16 vols. Burdett, NY: Larson Publications, 1984-1988. Comprehensive, detailed presentation of virtually all aspects of the Perennial Philosophy, from one of the pioneers of this century's spiritual renaissance of the West.

Bucke, Richard M. *Cosmic Consciousness*. Secaucus, NJ: University Books, 1961 (1901). A brilliant and still relevant study of the enlightenment experiences of many individuals throughout history, including ordinary Americans in the nineteenth century. It is liberating to see how common the experience of awakening has been.

Capra, Fritjof. *The Turning Point*. New York: Simon & Schuster, 1982. One of the first systematic surveys of the "New Paradigm" of a holistic, ecological, spiritual world-view integrating academics, the sciences, and spirituality.

————. *The Web of Life*. New York: Anchor/Doubleday, 1996. Thoughtful presentation of deep ecology and the holistic, systems view of life.

Chappell, Tom. *The Soul of a Business: Managing for Profit and the Common Good*. New York: Bantam, 1993. How the head of Tom's of Maine combined shrewd business sense and a Harvard degree in theology to cultivate lasting values and spirituality in a successful business.

Chardin, Pierre Teilhard de. *The Phenomenon of Man*. New York: Harper & Row, 1959. A brilliant, prophetic, visionary survey of the spiritual evolution of humanity and the earth, integrating evolutionary science and Christian revelation. Teilhard, a mystical Jesuit paleontologist, saw humanity moving toward a common, unifying global consciousness.

Covey, Stephen R. *The Seven Habits of Highly Effective People.* New York: Fireside, 1989. A highly principled look at the power of paradigms, values, and beliefs in the development of character as the basis for effective living. This longtime bestseller touched a spiritual nerve in our culture.

Csikszentmihaly, Mihaly. *Flow: The Psychology of Optimal Experience.* New York: Harper & Row, 1990. A comprehensive study of the flow experience integrating psychological and spiritual aspects, drawing on a wide range of examples, with suggestions on how to live the optimal experience in daily life.

Davis, Martha, et al. *The Relaxation and Stress Reduction Workbook.* Oakland: New Harbinger, 1982. Excellent workbook of techniques.

Dass, Ram. *Be Here Now.* New Mexico: Lama Foundation, 1971.

————. *Journey of Awakening.* New York: Bantam, n.d.

———— and Paul Gorman. *How Can I Help?: Stories and Reflections on Service.* New York: Knopf, 1985.

———— and Mirabai Bush. *Compassion in Action: Setting Out on the Path of Service.* New York: Bell Tower, 1992. Ram Dass (Richard Alpert) turned on a whole generation to the inner world of consciousness and transcendence. He has been one of America's most beloved spiritual teachers and clearest proponents of the Perennial Philosophy since his revolutionary *Be Here Now* became a spiritual handbook for contemporary seekers. Later works detailed both the practical and philosophical aspects of experiencing spirituality in everyday life.

Deshimaru, Taisen. *The Ring of the Way.* New York: E.P. Dutton, 1983. Succinct statement of the essence of Zen in the tradition of Dogen by a contemporary Japanese master.

The Dhammapada. Edited by Juan Mascaró. New York: Penguin, 1973. Translation from the Pali of aphorisms of ancient Buddhist teachings on the "path of perfection."

Eckhart, Meister. *Meister Eckhart.* Translated by Raymond Blakney. New York: Harper & Row, 1944. Eckhart, the towering giant of medieval Catholic mysticism, describes the heart of the non-dual realization in a uniquely Christian language that is universal in its approach.

Emerson, Ralph Waldo. *The Selected Writings of Ralph Waldo Emerson.* Edited by Brooks Atkinson. New York: Random House, 1940.

————. *Selections from Ralph Waldo Emerson.* Edited by Stephen E. Whicher. Boston: Houghton Mifflin, 1960. I felt immediate kinship with Emerson's lifelong attempt to integrate the spiritual in everyday American life. A true American sage in the non-dual tradition,

Emerson expresses an enlightened vision that is equally relevant today as it was in his own time.

Emery, Marcia. *Intuition Workbook.* n.p.: Prentice-Hall, 1994.

———. *The Power of Intuition* (tape). 1997. Dr. Marcia Emery's books and tapes are excellent practical introductions to the uses of intuition and practices for accessing our deeper wisdom.

Fanning, Patrick. *Visualization for Change.* Oakland, CA: New Harbinger, 1982. Practical manual on the uses of visualization in a wide variety of applications.

Frost, Robert. *The Poetry of Robert Frost.* Edited by Edward C. Lathem. New York: Holt, Rinehart & Winston, 1969. An American classic of great spiritual depth.

Garfield, Charles. *Peak Performers.* New York: William Morrow, 1986. In-depth study of key characteristics and practices of peak performers in many fields.

Geldard, Richard. *The Esoteric Emerson: The Spiritual Teachings of Ralph Waldo Emerson.* Hudson, NY: Lindisfarne, 1993. A deep plunge into the mystical core of Emerson's experience and teachings.

Gershon, David, and Gail Straub. *Empowerment.* New York: Delta, 1989. A useful introduction and practical workbook approach to the guidelines and techniques of personal empowerment. Emphasizes the power of mind, identifying and transforming belief systems, the tools of affirmation and visualization in many areas of our lives.

Goleman, Daniel. *The Meditative Mind.* Los Angeles: Tarcher, 1988. Good introduction to a wide variety of meditation techniques from throughout the world.

Gozdz, Kazimierz, ed. *Community Building: Renewing Spirit and Learning in Business.* San Francisco: New Leaders Press, 1995. Excellent collection of articles by leading experts on many dimensions of community in the development of more conscious organizations.

Hanh, Thich Nhat. *The Miracle of Mindfulness: A Manual in Meditation.* Boston: Beacon, 1965. Excellent practical instruction in the practice of mindfulness.

———. *Being Peace.* Berkeley, CA: Parallax, 1987. A classic of spiritual guidance from a living Buddhist master.

Houghton, James R. "The Growth Imperative: A Call to Leadership and Values." Speech to the Corporate Management Group, Corning Incorporated, January 1994. The former CEO of Corning makes a heartfelt statement of the power of values in transforming the company.

Huang Po. *The Zen Teachings of Huang Po.* New York: Grove, 1958. One of my first teachers, this ancient Chinese Zen master throws lightning bolts of wisdom that clarify the simplicity of being awake.

Hurley, Thomas J., III. "Altruistic Spirit Program." *Noetic Sciences Review,* No. 5, Winter, 1987, 11-16. On the Institute of Noetic Sciences' promotion of altruistic service and the power of compassion.

Huxley, Aldous. *The Perennial Philosophy.* New York: Harper & Row, 1970. The classic, masterful study of the perennial wisdom and unitive consciousness with quotes from the major world religions and mystics that show the underlying similarities.

Insight Consulting Group. "Managing Accelerated Performance." Follow-up material [workshop], 1986. Excellent understanding of how belief systems, declaration, and visualization work as the basis for effective time management and high performance.

Jackson, Phil, and Hugh Delehanty. *Sacred Hoops: Spiritual Lessons of a Hardwood Warrior.* New York: Hyperion, 1995. Fascinating account of Phil Jackson's own spiritual life and how the coach introduced meditation and spiritual awareness to the NBA champion Chicago Bulls.

Jaworski, Joseph. *Synchronicity: The Inner Path of Leadership.* San Francisco: Berret-Koehler, 1996. Son of Leon Jaworski, former Watergate special prosecutor, describes his personal transformation into an inner-directed leader and how new thinking is redefining our view of leadership today.

Kabir. *The Kabir Book.* Translated by Robert Bly. Boston: Beacon, 1977.

————. *Songs of Kabir.* Translated by R. Tagore. New York: Samuel Weiser, 1977. The ecstatic, playful, mystical poetry of the great fifteenth-century Indian saint Kabir. Expresses both the Hindu and Sufi traditions of the *bhakti* path of the union of the Lover and Beloved at the heart of the Perennial Philosophy.

Klein, Jean. *The Ease of Being.* Durham, NC: Acorn, 1984.

————. *I Am.* Santa Barbara, CA: Third Millenium, 1989. A Swiss Advaita master, formerly a musicologist and doctor, Klein describes the process and experience of his awakening to full self-awareness. His direct approach emphasizes silent awareness, unconditional acceptance, and full feeling attention in the here and now.

Krishnamurti, J. *The First and Last Freedom.* New York: Harper & Row, 1954.

————. *Krishnamurti's Notebook.* New York: Harper & Row, 1976. Penetrating, succinct descriptions of a streamlined, no-nonsense, non-dual consciousness by one of the century's great sages.

Lao Tzu. *The Way of Life According to Lao Tzu.* Translated by Witter Bynner. New York: Putnam, 1944. My favorite, poetic translation of the great Chinese classic of awakened living, one of the most translated books in the world, which effortlessly integrates profound consciousness, sage advice on leadership, and practical suggestions for simple living in harmony with the way of life. John Mabry's book includes another translation (see below).

Mabry, John R. *God as Nature Sees God: A Christian Reading of the Tao Te Ching.* Rockport, MA: Element Inc., 1994. A lucid, gender-inclusive translation Lao Tzu's *Tao Te Ching,* with valuable commentary on parallels between Christianity and Taoism.

MacDonald, Copthorne. *Toward Wisdom: Finding Our Way to Inner Peace, Love and Happiness.* Ontario, Canada: Hounslow, 1993. Thorough and wise approach to the common wisdom themes of the world's spiritual, philosophical, psychological, and scientific traditions by a former engineer.

Maslow, Abraham. *Religions, Values, and Peak-Experiences.* New York: Viking-Penguin, 1978. One of the classics on self-actualization and self-transcendence from a western point of view.

Muggeridge, Malcolm. *Something Beautiful for God: Mother Teresa of Calcutta.* Garden City: Doubleday, 1977. An up-close, moving, realistic portrait of a true saint in everyday life and how her deeply mystical vision infused her daily work.

Nachmanovitch, Stephen. *Free Play: The Power of Improvisation in Life and the Arts.* n.p.: Putnam/Tarcher, 1991.

———. "The Creative Moment. Mind at Play." *Intuition,* Vol. 2, No. 1, Issue 5 (1995). A musician and student of creativity, Nachmanovitch brilliantly integrates a transcendental spiritual vision and understanding of non-dual consciousness into his deep, wide-ranging study of play and improvisation.

Nisargadatta Maharaj, Sri. *I Am That.* Translated by Maurice Frydman. Durham, NC: Acorn, 1973.

———. *Seeds of Consciousness.* Edited by Jean Dunn. Durham, NC: Acorn, 1982. The Maharaj, a modern Indian awakened master (1897-1981) presents a compelling, passionate picture of the supreme consciousness that has touched thousands of spiritual seekers around the world.

Noer, David M. *Healing the Wounds: Overcoming the Trauma of Layoffs and Revitalizing Downsized Organizations.* San Francisco: Jossey-Bass, 1993. Moving description of the effects of downsizing and positive approaches to enhance the morale and well-being of survivors.

Pattakos, Alex, and Roger Frantz. *Intuition at Work.* San Francisco: New Leaders Press, 1997. Collection of essays on the many dimensions of intuition and consciousness in work and business.

Pert, Candace B. *Molecules of Emotion.* New York: Scribner, 1997. Research in mindbody studies and psychoneuroimmunology.

Poonja, Sri H.W.L. *Wake Up and Roar,* 1992-93, 2 vols. Kula, HI: Pacific Center. The first publication of selected satsangs with Papaji.

———. *Papaji: Interviews.* Edited by David Godman. Boulder, CO: Avadhuta, 1993. Interviews, mostly by western students and journalists, with Papaji, giving a clear presentation of his teachings and life. Skillfully edited by his student and outstanding scholar David Godman.

———. *The Truth Is.* Lucknow, India, 1995. A superb edition and selection of Papaji's key teachings through his *satsangs*—questions and answers with his students—that presents the best picture of this master of the Indian Advaita tradition.

Rabbin, Robert. "The Koan of Leadership," in John Renesch, ed., *Leadership in a New Era: Visionary Approaches to the Biggest Crisis of Our Time.* San Francisco: Berret-Koehler, 1994. Profound, subtle view of leadership from the non-dual perspective. Rabbin's work expresses a pure, authentic vision.

Ramana Maharshi. *Be As You Are: The Teachings of Sri Ramana Maharshi.* Edited by David Godman. New York; Viking/Penguin, 1992. A lucid and informed translation of Ramana Maharshi's teachings by one of the foremost western students of the Advaita approach. The Maharshi, a beacon of enlightenment, was one of India's best known and most widely loved sages of the twentieth century.

Ray, Paul H. "The Rise of Integral Culture." *Noetic Sciences Review,* no. 37 (Spring, 1996), 5-15. Demographic and historical account of the rise of a sector of the U.S. population engaged in spiritual, holistic, ecological way of life.

Renesch, John, ed. *Leadership in a New Era: Visionary Approaches to the Biggest Crisis of Our Time.* San Francisco: Berret-Koehler, 1994. Anthology of writings by leading thinkers on leadership, organizations, and consciousness.

Renesch, John, and Bill DeFoore. *The New Bottom Line: Bringing Heart and Soul to Business.* San Francisco: Sterling & Stone/New Leaders Press, 1996. Excellent anthology by leading consultants and business people on the relevance of spirituality, values, love, self-discovery, consciousness and healing in the business and corporate world.

Rossman, Martin, M.D. *Healing Yourself: A Step-by-Step Program for Better Health through Imagery.* New York: Walker, 1987. Practical, detailed description of how to use imagery for health and well-being.

Rumi, Jalal al-Din. *The Essential Rumi.* Translated by Coleman Barks. New York: Harper, 1995. Generally considered the greatest mystical poet in Islam, this thirteenth-century Sufi dervish, saint, teacher, and philosopher exquisitely expresses the ecstasy of enlightenment.

Russell, Peter. *The Global Brain Awakens: Our Next Evolutionary Leap,* 2nd ed. Palo Alto, CA: Global Brain, 1995. Inspired discussion of the evolution of society, technology, and consciousness toward a greater awakening of a planetary consciousness, with reflections on the role of the Internet and global telecommunications in an emerging global brain.

Scherer, John, with Larry Shook. *Work and the Human Spirit.* Spokane, WA: John Scherer, 1993. Consultant John Scherer's personal experiences and his work coaching executives confirmed for me that nurturing the human spirit is essential to organizational survival, and gave me a model for integrating spirit and work.

Scholem, Gershom G. *Major Trends in Jewish Mysticism.* New York: Schocken, 1941. A magnificent, scholarly, and wise study of the uniqueness of Jewish mysticism and, by implication, the universal aspects that it shares with the Perennial Philosophy and non-dual consciousness.

Seung, Sahn. *Only Don't Know: The Zen Letters of Zen Master Seung Sahn.* San Francisco: Four Seasons, 1982. Direct, intimate, encouraging letters to students about living Zen in daily life from a Korean Zen master and founder of the Providence Zen Center and related centers throughout the U.S. and world.

Siegel, Bernie. *Love, Medicine and Miracles.* New York: Harper & Row, 1986. A classic, personal, moving account by a surgeon and oncologist of his experiences working with cancer patients. Brilliant description of holistic mind-body studies and the power of love in the healing process.

Simonton, O. Carl, Stephanie Matthews-Simonton, and James L. Creighton. *Getting Well Again.* New York: Bantam, 1980. Groundbreaking study of the Simontons' successful use of mind-body healing techniques in their Cancer Counseling and Research Center. They inspired new research and practice in the use of mental-emotional techniques in healing.

Smothermon, R. *Winning through Enlightenment.* San Francisco. Context, 1980. An in-your-face presentation of approaches to "getting it" in the *est* style.

Spangler, David. *Manifestation: The Inner Art.* Morningtown, 1988. A modern American prophet and mystic, Spangler draws on the ancient wisdom in his practical suggestions for creating one's experience and life.

Suzuki, Shunryu. *Zen Mind, Beginner's Mind.* New York: Weatherhill, 1970. My first introduction to Zen, this simple description of meditation and clarity by the beloved founder of the San Francsico Zen Center inspired many to focus on the truth within.

Tapscott, Don. "Leadership for the Internetworked Business." *InformationWeek,* November 13, 1995, 65-72.

———. *The Digital Economy: Promise and Peril in the Age of Networked Intelligence.* New York: McGraw-Hill, 1996. Tapscott discusses new forms of leadership and work in the networked computer age.

Trungpa, Chögyam. *The Myth of Freedom.* Boston: Shambhala, 1976.

———. *Shambhala: The Sacred Path of the Warrior.* Boulder: Shambhala, 1985. Trungpa, an Oxford-educated Tibetan Buddhist Master, founded the Naropa Institute in Boulder and translated the profound Tibetan teachings on enlightenment and living skillfully for his contemporary American students.

Turkle, Sherry. *The Second Self: Computers and the Human Spirit.* New York: Simon & Schuster, 1984.

———. *Life on the Screen: Identity in the Age of the Internet.* New York: Simon & Schuster, 1995. Insightful studies and reflections on the pervasive impact of computers and cyberspace on modern society, with profound insight into the psychological and spiritual dimensions of who we think we are and how we live. Very rich fare.

The Upanishads. Edited by Juan Mascaró. New York: Penguin, 1965. Translation of selected great Sanskrit spiritual treatises of ancient India that give succinct expressions of the unitive consciuousness.

Whitman, Walt. *Leaves of Grass.* New York: Modern Library, [1855]. An authentic, enlightened American sage gives a unique, exuberant New World flavor to the perennial wisdom in this unabashedly lyrical poetry.

Walsh, Roger. "Perennial Wisdom in a Postmodern World." *Inquiring Mind,* 12:1 (Fall 1995), 6-8. Updating the Perennial Philosophy.

Watts, Alan. *The Wisdom of Insecurity.* New York: Panetheon, 1951. Watts reveals the wisdom that yields true security in an age of insecurity.

———. *The Book on the Taboo against Knowing Who You Are.* New York: Vintage, 1966. Watts gives us a modern, western explanation, spiced with his usual wit and lucidity, of the ancient wisdom of the Indian Vedas that cuts through the illusion of the separate individual to the underlying Self of the universe.

Wheatley, Margaret J. *Leadership and the New Science.* San Francisco: Berret-Koehler, 1992. A breakthough book, winner of the best business book of its year, describes the relevance of new thinking in quantum physics, evolution, whole systems, information, and other new sciences to a radical view of leadership and organizations.

———. "The Unplanned Organization." *Noetic Sciences Review,* no. 37 (Spring 1996), 16-23. Insightful talk on creativity, self-organization, and change in nature and the implications for organizations.

Wheatley, Margaret J. and Myron Kellner-Rogers. *A Simpler Way.* San Francisco: Berret-Koehler, 1996. Beautiful, philosophical look at leadership, organizations, life, and consciousness, suggesting a playful, joyful, openness to learning in harmony with the self-emergent flow of change and new possibilities.

Whyte, David. *The Heart Aroused: Poetry and the Preservation of the Soul in Corporate America.* New York: Currency/Doubleday, 1994. Lyrical and penetrating insight by a poet using poetry to plumb the depths of spiritual awakening and the possibilities for well-being in the midst of corporate life today. Shows a range of paths to satisfy the deep longing for meaning, transcendence and joy in the workplace.

Wilber, Ken. *The Spectrum of Consciousness.* Wheaton, IL: Quest, 1977.

———. *No Boundary: Eastern and Western Approaches to Personal Growth.* Los Angeles: Center, 1980.

———. *A Brief History of Everything.* Boston: Shambhala, 1996. Considered "the Einstein of consciousness studies," Wilber brilliantly integrates the essence of the world wisdom paths to wholeness and self-realization. A longtime student and spiritual practitioner, he provides lucid explanations of the nature and development of unitive consciousness.

Wolf, Fred Alan. *Star Wave: Mind Consciousness and Quantum Physics.* New York: Macmillan, 1984. Reflections by a physicist on the mysteries and connections of physics and consciousness.